CHARLES W. STECKEL

DESTRUCTION AND SURVIVAL

"Love, work and knowledge are the well-springs of our life. They should also govern it."

Wilhelm Reich

Ignorance, hatred and prejudice are the well-springs of all evil. They ought to be eradicated.

Charles W. Steckel

DEDICATED
to
FRANCES REITMAN CAPLAN
Who, Like the Biblical Woman of Valor, Follows
The Principle of Doing Justly, of Loving Mercy,
And of Walking Humbly with God.

and
to

THE LATE JOSEPH CAPLAN
Who, Like the Ancient Teachers, Combined
In Himself Profound Love of Man With The
Scholar's Reverence for Law and Truth.

iii

Table of Contents

DESTRUCTION AND SURVIVAL

Table of Contents

IN TRIBUTE
To the Sainted Memory of
All Martyrs of the Holocaust,
Including My Mother, Brother, His Wife
and Daughter, and My Sisters,
Who Perished in Poland (Eastern Galicia)
During the Winter — Spring of 1943 (5703).

Acknowledgements

Parts of this book have appeared in different form in the YIVO Annual of Jewish Social Science, The Jewish Spectator and Judaism (1971-72).

I wish to express my appreciation to Dr. Shlomo Noble, YIVO INSTITUTE FOR JEWISH RESEARCH, New York, for his interest in this volume. My sincere thanks go to Mrs. Marie Wood for the valuable help in typing and retyping the manuscript. Mrs. Nettie Jacobs deserves my gratitude for giving freely of her time, assisting me in correcting the manuscript, and for making invaluable suggestions. Above and beyond all other help, I have had the active assistance and patient forbearance of my wife, Ilana H. Steckel.

I am grateful to the libraries of the Jewish Federation-Council and the University of Judaism in Los Angeles.

Special thanks are also due to Mrs. Frances R. Caplan, whose kind and persistent interest encouraged me to pursue this publication.

Charles W. Steckel

Foreword

"Auschwitz" is the name of the most infamous place on earth. It is also a generic term for the many "Auschwitzes" of the holocaust. Dr. Steckel's "Auschwitz" was Osijek, where he served as a rabbi, and Sarajewo, Tenje and Jasenovac, where he and his Community were involved. He and his wife survived — but his mother, his brother and his family, and his sisters perished with millions of martyrs in Poland.

Some weeks ago, I told friends who are raising funds for City of Hope Medical Center that I see meaning in Dr. Steckel serving as Chaplain of City of Hope. As all survivors of the holocaust, he is alive because of HOPE, the belief and confidence that good will win out in "the end of days" (aharit hayamim), which is, in fact, a new beginning in the here-and-now — Not in heaven!

Dr. Steckel knows that forty-four million human beings perished as a result of the Nazi madness which led to World War II — in addition to six million Jews. He also knows that the Machiavellian spirit is still guiding those who govern the big and the small nations. He knows that one third of our Jewish people were murdered — no other people suffered losses even slightly comparable — because Washington and London, the Vatican and American Jews were *silent*. He knows that not all Jews who perished in the holocaust were heroes. Some even tried (few succeeded) to save themselves at the expense of others. Rabbi Steckel knows that humans can be but little lower than the angels. He remembers the goodness of many "angelic" men and women — Jews and Christians — and he does not gloss over the misdeeds of "devilish" Jews and Christians, and the callousness of those who accuse the Six Million of having walked to their deaths "like sheep to the slaughter."

In Europe, a rabbi is customarily referred to as a *Theologe*. Rabbi Steckel is well versed in theology, also "Holocaust Theologies". But for him, the holocaust is not a theological problem of theodicy. Not God but Roosevelt and Churchill and the Pope were "silent". Not God but men and women were "in hiding" so as not to see. They did not act when children, and babes in their mothers' arms, were cruelly tortured and brutally battered to death.

There is no theological basis for a theodicy of the holocaust because "the earth has been given to the children of man". Being capable of freely choosing either the good or the evil is what sets humans apart from the primates. Men — not God — lord it *in* the world. God did not die in Auschwitz, nor was Auschwitz the cause of what some theologians term the hiding of God.

It was NOT God's will that millions died of contagious diseases which now have been conquered by medical science. It was superstition and the taboo of the inviolability of the human body (hence no autopsies) which kept medicine from progressing. It is NOT God's will that millions die of cancer every year but the horrendously misguided waste of hundreds of billions on war — resources, if invested in medical research, would surely result in the same break-through that rewarded the crash-and-no-expense-spared nuclear and space programs.

According to Dr. Steckel not God but "ignorance, hatred and prejudice are the well-springs of all evil". This is why "they ought to be eradicated".

There is too little knowledge about the holocaust, especially among those under forty. But facts and data alone are not really "knowledge". Part II of "Destruction and Survival" is a major addition to the facts and data of the holocaust. But of equal, and *sub specie aeternitatis*, greater significance, are the two parts of the book mostly taken up with Rabbi Steckel's reflections on the *Destruction* and the *Survival* — the survival of the vision of "peace" . . . "the ultimate ideal" and "the hopeful quest".

Miracles — such is the consensus of the best Jewish minds — do not require suspension of the laws of nature. Miracles, or rather what is considered miraculous, are structured into nature. People will say it is "a miracle" when a man who has suffered as Rabbi Steckel has suffered and who has seen what he has seen, avows that there survives "the hope which gives meaning to all that passes". But those who are steeped in Jewishness, as Rabbi Steckel is, will consider it *natural* to hope and strive and work for "a remote possibility" which is "yet within our reach", the possibility of swords being made into ploughshares in the this-worldly future when men will not make war anymore, knowing that "Auschwitz" destroys also its makers.

Trude Weiss-Rosmarin

Introduction

It has become increasingly evident during the last decade that a great deal of material concerning the Holocaust is still buried in archives and private hands. Today, twenty-seven years after the end of World War II, new publications — in many languages — appear, almost daily. The author of this volume translated and edited new material which was never published before. History-Making Letters, Part II of this book, will aid the historian. He will be able to study, analyze and interpret Nazi-Ustashi oppression, having at his disposal authentic material.

William L. Shirer quoted* the ancient Greek historian Thucydides, who wrote in The History of the Peleponnesian War: "I lived through the whole War . . . being of an age to comprehend events and giving attention to them in order to know the exact truth about them." Mutatis mutandur, the author survived the Holocaust — lived during 1939-1945 in Yugoslavia and Hungary, and visited Slovakia and Rumania. I tried to be objective, letting the facts, as I saw and experienced them, speak for themselves and attempted to provide the historian with the source of the events. Everything described in this volume is based on fact. The incidents are based on documents, personal notes of the crucial years, the testimony of eyewitnesses and my own personal observations.

The author hopes that the essays, Part III of the book, will contribute to the clarification and re-evaluation of Holocaust Literature. The aims of Holocaust historians today should be — next to publishing of new books — a systematic and methodical arrangement of material already published centered around: 1, Historiography, 2, The Psycho-Philosophical Thought, 3, The Religio-Theological Aspect and 4, The Imaginative Literature (Prose and Poetry) of the Holocaust.

The aims of Holocaust historians today are, as I see them, fourfold: 1, To explain why some of the historians oversimplified facts and could not have been objective. To clarify why they could not have met all criteria of historiography at the time when they wrote their dissertations. Knowing half of the truth, is like not

*The Rise and Fall of the Third Reich, Crest Books A522, Fawcet World Library, New York, p. xii.

1

knowing it at all. 2, To explain areas where the goal of objectivity could not have been achieved. First, because "the dust had to settle." Second, the buried material had to be published. Third, the American and European archives had to become available. 3, What can we assess as being certain? What do we really know, understand and can truthfully say about the victims and perpetrators of the heinous crime? 4, What is the Lesson for Humanity and the Jewish People which we can learn from the Holocaust?**

It is said: history does not repeat itself. One has every right to doubt whether this statement is correct. The writer fully realizes that it would have been much easier to publish the material included in this volume (as well as the part which had to be deleted) in two separate books. However printing expenses, etc., did not permit this kind of arrangement.

To simplify the spelling and pronunciation of Serbo-Croatian words and names the English transliteration is being used.

**Holocaust is the term used to describe the annihilation of European Jewry during the years 1939-1945. Webster's dictionary defines holocaust as complete destruction of people or animals by fire.

PART I
From Spain To Bosnia

From Spain To Bosnia

In 1966, immediately after Sukkoth, the Jews of Bosnia and Herzegovina celebrated — as did the Federation of Jewish Communities of Yugoslavia — 400 years of organized Jewish communal life in Bosnia. For four days, from October 14 to 17, the Sherit Hapleta, remnant of once prominent Sephardic and Ashkenazic communities were in a festive but somber mood, remembering and meditating on the past. Sarajevo remembered for the second time within a century, that tragedy can begin in one place, at a given day, and spread in no time like pestilence over all continents.

The Jewish Spaniards of Bosnia, although decimated, take great pride in their glorious and tragic history. Those who decided to return to the ruins of their former homes and to remain there showed indestructible Will to Rise from the ashes and ruins of slaughter as if "flying on eagles' wings." They have proven that the urge to build again, "to run and not to be weary" (Isaiah 40, 31) is

very much alive in them as it was in their ancestors, who came
from Spain to live in Bosnia more than four centuries ago. The
eruption of the volcano of prejudice in Spain and Portugal at the
end of the fifteenth century, directed by the Inquisition, differed
basically from the sudden outburst of violence in 1941 in Croatia,
directed by the Ustashi. The Jews of Spain had been able to
emigrate. They were invited to settle in the empire of Sultan
Suleiman the Magnificent while the Jews of Bosnia had no place to
go. No invitation was extended to them to settle in any other
country. We should remember and be mindful of this fact when
we speak of the "dark middle ages." If the medieval period of
human history was dark, then the twentieth century was black and
sinister. The Inquisition was satisfied with the destruction of the
soul. It sought and accepted converts, while Nazism-Fascism-
Ustashism did not rest until the body was completely destroyed
physically.

The Sephardic Jews of Bosnia, particularly, remind us of the
people living in villages adjacent to the volcano Etna. The volcano
erupts frequently, causing destruction and death among the
villagers. Yet amazingly the villagers run back to their villages as
soon as the volcanic eruption has subsided and the lava has cooled.
They dig, remove destruction and ashes, and start life once again
as if nothing has happened. A new chapter begins immediately;
homes are built, gardens are cultivated and schools are erected.
What the lava of the volcano destroyed is now past history. Hope
and prayer inspire them to build again and they trust the tragedy
will not repeat itself. It makes survival less difficult and the
building of a future possible. All volcanos have this in common,
they enrich human experience and make men aware of their
unpredictable existence. Spain and Bosnia were in a sense unpredictable and taught the Sephardim as well as the Jewish people
a valuable lesson. Survival of any minority can not be taken for
granted even in our own generation, until the Messianic age will
eliminate the eruption of wars and volcanos of prejudice.

According to Dr. Moric Levi[1] , the last Sephardic Chief Rabbi of
Sarajevo, (tortured in Jasenovac, ordered back to Sarajevo and
Zagreb, then returned to the camp) — inscriptions on tombstones
at Sarajevo bear the Jewish date of 5311 or 1551 C.E.

According to other historians, the first Jews settled in Bosnia in

[1] Die Sephardim in Bosnien, 1911.

1575. Don Joseph Nasi of Naxos, and his aunt Dona Gracia, used their influence with the Sultan Suleiman the Magnificent, who permitted the newly arrived Spanioles to take residence in the province of Bosnia. It is evident from a manuscript written in Turkish and preserved in the Mohammedan library of Sarajevo that a small group of 30 to 40 Jews, was engaged in business at Bosna-Sarai (the present Sarajevo) under the Governor, Hadim-Ali-Bey, in the year 958 of the Hegira, or 1541 C.E. These merchants lived part of the year in Sarajevo and part of the year in Salonica. They were guided by the Hebrew calendar and joined their families — who resided permanently in Salonica — for holidays and festivals.

At the beginning of the 17th century, the Sephardim of Sarajevo were scattered in various districts of the city. They obtained in 1647 permission from the Governor Siavous Pasha to reside in a special quarter where they built permanent houses. A special decree (firman) granted them permission to establish a cemetery on a hill called Verbania. In this way the Jews definitely established themselves in Bosnia and other localities, as well as in Sarajevo.

In 1850 Omar Pasha granted the Jews of Sarajevo the right to settle in any part of the city. Until 1878, when the Austro-Hungarian monarchy took possession of Bosnia, the Jews living in Sarajevo, as well as throughout Bosnia and Herzegovina, were all Sephardim (Spanioles) speaking Ladino at home and synagogue. After 1878 an Ashkenazic congregation was established in the city. Its members were recruited from Jews who came from Austrian provinces or Hungary proper, after the monarchy's occupation of Bosnia. The last Ashkenazic Chief-Rabbi of Sarajevo, Dr. Hinko Urbach, avoided persecution by escaping to Italy and returned after the War to Yugoslavia. He and his family migrated to Israel in 1948. The Ashkenazim and Sephardim maintained a cordial relationship under the influence of the Zionist movement. Hebraism and Zionism went hand in hand and the Zionist Organization was often praised at Zionist Congresses for its vitality, leadership and aliya.

The Sephardim remained Spaniards, but divorced themselves from Spain, the land of Sepharad. There is no doubt that they left the Iberian peninsula with their feelings and hopes injured to the depths. According to one legend, the Sephardim pronounced a solemn herem (ban) on Spain never again to step on her soil. This

describes vividly how they felt. According to another legend the
Sephardim of Spain, when they left, dug the gravestones out of
the soil of the cemetery and took them along. They wanted future
generations to know how they departed from the land of ingrati-
tude. Gratitude was as much a part of their history and existence
as the blood in their veins was a part of their very lives. The
emotions, however, were too strong to conceal disappointment
and bitterness. For fifteen hundred years their names and reputa-
tion as physicians, merchants, bankers, artisans, and above all as
loyal citizens, had been spotless. Their communities had been
places of honor, fame and glory. And now all this was no longer
true. Their desire, hope and plan was to begin a new chapter in a
new land. To rise from the ashes of Destruction, to build again,
was their new mission. "To run and not to be weary" was their
aim and goal.

Mr. Selvyn Levi, husband of the principal of our parochial
school in Osijek, Luci Levi, and I approached the wife of a Haham,
interned at the Djakovo camp, informing her about a possibility of
obtaining a visa for her and her two boys to leave for Spain. She
answered calmly in perfect Hebrew: "I am sure that you are aware
of our tradition concerning Spain. We Sephardim adhere to a ban
never again to reside in the land of Sepharad. If you can prove to
me — through the signature of three Rabbis — that the ban has
been lifted, then I will sign the application for a Spanish visa."
"This is a time of great crisis and danger," I replied, "and quick
action is mandatory." The woman thought for a while, as if she
would be searching her heart, mind and soul. Finally she said to
us: "I know that my husband would have wanted me to say to
you, 'Please, let two elders of the Jewish Community sign their
names next to yours, Rabbi.' Under these circumstances Sephardim will again step upon the soil of the land of Sepharad." The
Spanish Embassy in Budapest was reluctant to issue a collective
visa for women and children under the age of 16 and the whole
matter was dropped. The courageous wife of the Haham and her
boys perished in Jasenovac. They were murdered by the Ustashi
guards of the infamous camp. Jasenovac, once a Serbian settlement, was situated off the railway line Zagreb-Belgrade, where the
river Una joins the river Sava. Victims murdered in Jasenovac
numbered between five hundred thousand and six hundred thousand. Among them were: Serbs, Croats, anti-Fascists and twenty
thousand Jews.

1

Yugoslavia's Pluralistic Jewry

Small in number, the Yugoslavian Jewry was colorful and in a sense pluralistic. Even the Sephardim were comprised of several groups. The Ashkenazim represented former Austrian, Hungarian, Central and East European Jews. The Jews spoke Serbo-Croatian, Ladino, German, Hungarian, Hebrew, as well as other languages. The Yugoslav Jews were quite progressive. There were parochial elementary schools and orthodox yeshivot, also a Seminary training hahamim-hazanim (spiritual leaders-cantors) for small congregations. The Seminary in Sarajevo graduated Hebrew speaking teachers for students attending gymnasia, and leaders for youth movements. Because of strong Zionist convictions and ideology, the barrier between the Sephardim and Ashkenazim disappeared completely. Marriages between the two groups were frequent. The younger generation could not help but wonder why the Ashkenazi Jew was called in Ladino, "Tudesco," and vice versa, why the Sephardi Jew should be treated as an outsider. The Hungarian-

9

speaking Jewry had some difficulties in switching from an Ugro-Finn to a Slavic language. The difficulties disappeared as young people went to gymnasia or universities. It was indeed a poly-lingual Jewry. Two and often three languages were spoken at home.

Yugoslavia's Jewry was prosperous and charitable. Outstanding physicians, engineers, lawyers, teachers were among them. Jews from Poland and Czechoslovakia, who settled there after 1918, helped to industrialize Croatia. The Chief Rabbi of the country was a persona grata and represented the Jewish Community in the Senate. Dr. Isaac Alkalay was able to leave Yugoslavia after the air attack on Belgrade on Sunday, April 6th, 1941, when six hundred Stukas devastated the capital and disrupted communication. Germany did not bother to declare War against Yugoslavia but rather initiated hostilities by bombing an open city because the people of the country refused to join the Axis.

Of the 75,500 Jews living in Yugoslavia in April 1941, 70,500 were Yugoslav Jews and citizens, while about 5,000 were emi-grants from Germany, Austria, Czechoslovakia and other sub-jugated countries. They found temporary asylum and refuge in the country and were cared for by the Union of Jewish Congregations. Besides the 117 Jewish Communities, there existed also a number of national, cultural, social and sport associations. Jewish libraries and archives, rich in collections of historical rarities, were the pride of a Jewish community which could trace the history of Jews living on the territory of the present Yugoslavia to the first century of C.E. Of the total number of 75,500 Jews in Yugoslavia only about 15,000 survived. More than 60,000 fell as martyrs; 9,000 emigrated to Israel; and about 6,500 are still living in the different parts of the country. Belgrade, Sarajevo and Zagreb remain the largest Jewish communities in the Federative People's Republic of Yugoslavia. Almost 2,000,000 Yugoslav citizens per-ished from April 1941 to May 1945, massacred by Germans, Ustashi and Volksdeutche.

The town of Djakovo (Djakovar in Hungarian) will be men-tioned frequently. This is the town where the idea of uniting all Southern Slavs was born. It originated with Bishop Josip J. Strossmayer, who served as house-teacher of the royal family in Vienna as a young Jesuit priest. He became the leading ideologist of a movement designed to unite all Serbs, Croats, Slovenes,

Montenegrins into one national state. To express his loyalty and belief in Pan-Slavism he wired from the capital of the monarchy to the Patriarch of the Greek Orthodox Church in Czarist Russia congratulating him on the 800th anniversary of the Eastern Church, only to be reprimanded for this by Kaiser Francis Joseph I himself for being disloyal to the monarch and the Hapsburgs.

Dr. Marcus Ehrenpreis, Rabbi of Djakovo, was co-editor of the famous Hebrew publication "Hashiloah". He used to substitute (as editor) for Ahad Ha-Am during the latter's long visits to Palestine. In the Igroth of Ahad Ha-Am Djakovar is mentioned frequently. Ehrenpreis later became — at the recommendation of Theodor Herzl — Chief-Rabbi of the Sephardic Community of Sofia (Bulgaria) and personal friend of the Bulgarian King. The Jewish Community of Djakovo kept letters and manuscripts pertaining to Ehrenpreis' rabbinic activity in a special safe during his residence there. He graciously left these as a personal gift to his flock before leaving for Sofia.

2

"The Independent
State of Croatia"

The Ante Pavelich Independent State of Croatia was granted independence by the Germans and guaranteed sovereignty by the Italians on April 10, 1941. The Duke of Spoleto, a kinsman of the Italian King Emanuel, was subsequently declared king of Croatia. The Jews in Bosnia-Herzegovina were especially hard hit as a result of the new political situation and the occupation by the German army. The local Moslems in the newly-formed state were inspired not only by the Ustashi but also by the former Grand Mufti of Jerusalem, Hadj Amin El Huseini. The new State decreed as early as April 18, 1941 that all property belonging to Jews was to be considered ownerless. Every legal right to possession was declared invalid, and all legal agreements between a Jew and a non-Jew were annulled. The purpose of this law was to speed up the process of taking over Jewish property and ownership of factories, shops and offices.

Pavelich's "Legal Decree and Order" on internment of Jews of June 26, 1941, stated that they "spread false news in order to alarm the population and by their notorious speculative methods rendered the supply for the population more difficult." The Legal Decree of November 23, 1941 said that "undesirable persons, dangerous for public order and security ... may be sent to concentration camps." From November, 1941 on, all Jews were treated as "undesirable and dangerous persons." Even protective certificates, signed by Pavelich himself exempting patriotic and indispensable Jews, were canceled.

There were not only scenes of terrible horrors in the Ustashi annihilation of Croatian Jewry — as well as the Serbian population — but also a kind of barbarism, which the Germans partly succeeded in hiding from their civilian population. Next to dehumanizing and savage acts of barbarism against the Jews, there is also a Greek dimension of the tragedy in this chapter of "man's inhumanity to man." Ante Pavelich as well as his Marshal Slavko Kvaternik were partners in a plan of brutal deeds. Hitler's most faithful admirers, however, did not follow the "Aryan doctrine" of a pure race. They were guilty of mixed marriages.

For a brief time false hope spread over Croatia, based on wishful thinking, and on the fact that quite a number of the leaders of the new state had either Jewish wives or relatives. How could such a state impose and practice the Nuremberg Laws? Both Pavelich and Kvaternik had Jewish wives. Among the assimilated Jews in Zagreb, the families of Lorencevich and Frank were prominent. The daughter of Lorencevich married Pavelich and the daughter of Frank became the wife of Kvaternik. Both women were practicing Roman Catholics. The marriage of the Kvaterniks was "blessed" with a son, Eugene (Dido) Kvaternik, who became State Secretary for Security. He united all police forces and powers in his bloody hands. What an irony that a descendant of a Jewish mother should become the blood thirsty executioner of her relatives! Eugene Kvaternik organized and executed the massacre of entire Greek Orthodox villages. The homes were burnt to cinders and the men, women and children were annihilated. His acts of atrocity forced the Italian and German army commanders to intervene in behalf of the Greek Orthodox victims. While the Croatian "Attila" made himself known as the executioner of innocent people, his distinguished father and first Marshal of the "independent State" was dismissed and exiled by Pavelich, after a short reign as Chief of the Army. Marshal Kvaternik found hospitality and friendship in Slovakia where the same kind of terror, which he helped to introduce in his native Croatia, reigned.

To be a Jew in Croatia in 1941 meant to suffer, to be helpless; but to be a Rabbi as well as the father of David Frankfurter, meant, since April 10, 1941, to experience Dante's inferno every minute. When David Frankfurter, who had tuberculosis of the bones and lived in Switzerland, assassinated the Nazi leader, Wilhelm Gustloff in Davos, on February 6, 1936, his saintly father, Dr. Mavro Frankfurter, Rabbi of Vinkovci, a neighboring community of Osijek, was the first one to condemn the violent act of his sickly son. Neither of them knew at that time that five years later Vinkovci would become the scene of revenge and bestiality against an innocent father, for the violence committed by his son, who was sentenced to eighteen years in prison by the Swiss court, on December 9, 1936. Mavro Frankfurter was ordered by German soldiers to stand on a table for days, while the soldiers would spit in his face, pull out the hair from his long beard or hit him with a rifle. Civilians, Ustashi as well as members of the Volksbund, participated in the "show." The spectacle lasted for weeks until he and others were taken to a concentration camp.

The three largest Kehiloth (Communities) — mentioned in the letters and minutes describing the annihilation of the Bosnian Jewry — were Zagreb, Sarajevo and Osijek. The Osijek Jewish Community, although the smallest of the three, played a very important role because of its proximity to Djakovo and the Hungarian border. Simultaneously with the arrest of Jews in the middle of April, 1941 extortion and plundering of Jewish property began. "Official contributions" were imposed by the German Army, through the Volksbund, to be paid collectively by individual Jewish Communities. Thus in Zagreb, Jews were forced to pay a "contribution" of 100 kilos of gold. In Osijek a number of leaders and wealthier Jews were arrested and held as hostages until the Community paid a "contribution" of 20 million Dinars. The spokesman for the Volksbund, Lutz, originally asked for 30 million Dinars (30 kilos gold) and eventually settled for 20 million. The Ustashi realized very soon that the Volksbund had no right to be the beneficiary of the spoils and demanded a lion's share of the "contribution." Eventually the spirit of comradeship prevailed and the "misunderstanding" was settled peacefully. Both parties, the Volksbund and the Ustashi, benefited from the imposed "contribution," and divided the spoils.

On April 16, 1941 the Germans entered Sarajevo. They broke into the main Jewish Temple together with a mob of the natives and after plundering it, demolished it. Not only were the library and valuable archives destroyed, but also the museum which contained works of great value. Smaller houses of worship suffered the same fate. The first internment of Sarajevo Jews took place at midnight on September 3, 1941. From the collection camp, the victims were later sent to the Krushica camp, 17 kms from Travnik. At the end of September, 1941 the camp was evacuated. Of the 3,000 persons interned in the camp, the men were transported to Jasenovac and the women and children were sent to Loborgrad.

The night of October 16th, 1941 a mass internment was carried out "in honor of the German Day." The night of November 15th, 1941 the largest mass arrest, comprising 3,000 persons, took place. Within less than five months, more than 8,500 Sarajevo Jews were arrested, interned and sent to concentration camps by the Utashi authorities. The last group of 120 persons, who were exempt and classified as experts or indispensable, lived in Sarajevo until August 12, 1942, when they were arrested and sent to Auschwitz. Of over 9,000 Sarajevo Jews sent to concentration camps, only 40 survived. Before the War approximately 14,000 Jews resided in Bosnia and Herzegovina. Twelve thousand of them perished during the occupation; 11,000 in Croatian concentration camps or in Auschwitz. Thus about 85% of the total number of the Jews living in pre-World War II Bosnia-Herzegovina were annihilated, regardless of sex, age or political ideology.

3

Distorted

Historiography

Despite George Hills and Rabbi Chaim Lifschitz,[2] who praise Generalissimo Francisco Franco for saving the (Spaniards) Sephardim of Bosnia, the fact remains that less than 15% of them escaped annihilation by being able to cross into the Italian sectors of occupied Yugoslavia, called Zone I, and by joining Tito's partisans. The coastal area of Dalmatia some fifty miles in depth, and the division of zones and sectors, played a vital role in the life and death struggle of Croatian Jews, including those of Bosnia.

In spring of 1970 Lifschitz stated in New York that Generalissimo Francisco Franco saved 60,000 European Jews during World War II by permitting them to enter Spain as refugees. Swiss, German and Italian periodicals and newspapers all over Europe

[2] George Hills, Franco the Man and His Nation, The MacMillan Company, New York, 1968, pp. 408-411.

16

and also Newsweek and Anglo-Jewish weeklies in our country printed this news item with no hesitation or previous inquiry as to the accuracy of this statement.

Los Angeles residents who were refugees in Spain during World War II questioned "the information and enthusiasm" displayed by Rabbi Lifschitz. They have been asked by the writer of this book to write depositions concerning their experience, which they described as harsh, in view of the fact that they had French passports and American visas. Sixty thousand Jewish refugees were presumably rescued by Franco. From where did they come? Very few could have come from Southern, Eastern or even Central Europe! Some could have reached Spain from Holland, France, or Belgium.

Renowned Jewish historians León Poliakov (Paris) and Jacob Presser (Amsterdam) report that some French (Vichy) and Dutch Jews were fortunate enough to avoid deportation and to cross illegally into Spain. But they represented a small number. Spain, on principle, did not admit male refugees between the ages of 18 and 41. Everyone who entered that country illegally was arrested and interned, for longer or shorter periods, in Miranda del Ebro camp. All those released had a period of forced residence in Madrid until they obtained a Portuguese visa. A letter to the Editor of B'nai B'rith Messenger, April 3, 1970, and a deposition to Rabbi C.W. Steckel, July 31, 1970, read:

April 3, 1970

Dear Sir:

Your article about Franco's kindness to the Jewish refugees during World War II surprised me and my family very much. My two brothers were jailed for several weeks in "Carcel Model" immediately after their entry into Spain in the beginning of 1943 though my older brother was already ill with TB. Both had the French passport for refugees from Germany and their visa to USA issued in Marseille. When they finally were allowed to go on to Portugal, it was already too late, because my older brother shortly died there after in a Portuguese Sanitarium.

Unfortunately the medal of the "Quiet Samaritan" has two sides. Rabbi Chaim Lifschitz from Brooklyn had one sided information. The enthusiasm cannot be shared by us.

Kindly let our good Rabbi know of our cruel experience. My accusation is not quiet.

Most sincerely yours,

Theophila Arnhein
11344 Berwick Street
Los Angeles, Calif. 90049

Theophila Arnhein/11344 Berwick St./Los Angeles, Calif.

July 31, 1970

Dear Rabbi:

In reply to your request of July 23 regarding the myth of Franco's kindness toward the Jews I want to give you the following details concerning my 2 brothers. Both were born in Warsaw, Poland and became later naturalized German citizens. They emigrated to France during the Nazi regime. Prior to World War II they received in exchange for turning in their German Passports from the French government the passport of "Refugié provenant d'Allemagne".

In 1942 they were able to receive a U.S. visa from the U.S. Consul in Marseille. They were then smuggled across the border of the Pyrenees so that they could go to the U.S. from Portugal.

Upon arrival in Spain in January 1943, they were immediately incarcerated and put into prison in Barcelona in spite of the fact that they wanted just to pass through to leave for America, and although my older brother of age 45 had evident T.B.

After several weeks they were released, but my older brother died in transit in Portugal because his condition had worsened due to the enforced daily cold showers in winter and the damp quarters in Carcel Modelo.

I hope this information is helpful to you, dear Rabbi.

Most sincerely yours,
(signed)   Theophila Arnhein

In spring 1942 a representative of the International Red Cross was on official business in Budapest. Sweden's cultural attaché, Valdemar Langlet, arranged a meeting between Yugoslav Jews and the Swiss emissary at the Ritz Hotel located on the Danube. Also the Spanish Embassy was approached to help women and children with Spanish names, such as Albala, Albahari, Finzi, Maestro, Romano, Toladino. The conversations with the International Red Cross emissary were discouraging and meaningless. He was evasive and vague as far as the intervention of the International Red Cross was concerned on behalf of Jewish refugees residing in Budapest under assumed names. There were also those who had not been registered with the Police at all. This created an additional difficulty for the refugees in renting lodgings and obtaining food rationing coupons. He was unwilling, despite all this, to intervene officially and to ask the Hungarian Government to implement the policy of protecting War refugees according to The Hague and Geneva conventions.

Rumors prevailed in winter and spring of 1942 that Franco's regime was interested in repatriating Sephardim with genuine Spanish names. There were others, also those descendants of Spaniards, who spoke Ladino. Women, children and elderly people would have preference.

To test the credibility of these rumors a delegation of four men asked for an appointment with the Spanish Embassy in Budapest. Albahari, who spoke fluently Spanish and Ladino, assisted by Dr. Francis Herzog, a Sephardi medical student from Belgrade, Atijas, and the author of this book, presented themselves as spokesmen. The delegation petitioned the Embassy for a collective visa for 9 women and 16 children (all under 16).

A diplomat, Valdemar Langlet, who was lecturer of the Swedish language at the University of Budapest and served as cultural attaché of the Swedish Embassy in Budapest—(later on, summer of 1944 he became the Head of the Swedish Red Cross in Hungary)—helped to write and formulate the legal aspect of the petition. He was in contact with the International Red Cross, which promised to obtain a transit visa and eventually to accompany the group. This group was transferred, from the camp in Djakovo, to the hospital in Osijek. The hospital would have released the refugees, provided they obtained a passport or visa. The answer Albahari received from the embassy read: "The

government of Spain sincerely regrets that the international
situation does not permit, at this time, to consider the petition in
the affirmative." This was in early spring of 1942. Spain could
have been a real blessing and a haven of refuge for the oppressed
Sephardim of Bosnia and Sarajevo.

The Italian practice, to process detailed registration according
to several categories of citizenship into which the refugees in the
Italian occupied territory were subdivided, was very helpful in the
struggle of saving lives of Jews. It resulted in gaining valuable time
and permitted the refugees to seek new contacts, often enabling
them to enter Italy proper. Many found their way into Italian
territory. Some Sarajevo Jews found refuge in Caltaro and Albania
which were under Italian occupation. The Protocol of Rome,
signed on June 13, 1941 between the Italian and Croatian Ustashi
Governments provided that the Italian occupation zone was
extended to include almost half of Croatia proper, Dalmatia and
Montenegro (Crna Gora). On March, 1943 the Italians began—
under German pressure and strong démarche in Rome—interning
Jewish refugees on the island of Rab (Arbe) and in the Gulf of
Arcarnero, off the coast of Croatia. The internment ended about
the same time that Mussolini was deposed by the new Government
of Marshal Badoglio. General Augusto Rosso, General-Secretary of
the Foreign Ministry, wired on August 19, 1943 urging the
Commander of the Italian Second Army not to surrender the
Croatian Jews under any circumstances. After the conclusion of
the armistice between the Allies and Italy, the Jews were freed
from the internment long before the War was over.

The Italian attitude and conduct towards Jews during World
War II—particularly towards refugees—is one of contradictory
praise and criticism. We have—in the first place—to distinguish
between two periods of the War. The years from 1939-1943
represent the first stage, while the second stage is marked by the
collapse of Mussolini's Government in summer 1943, the sign-
ing of the armistice, and ultimately the end of World War II.

Furthermore, geographical considerations and individual army
commanders played an important role. The civilian population and
the Italian clergy were as human and helpful as one can expect
under the circumstances. Joseph Tenenbaum writes in "Race and
Reich": "The saga of Italian generosity in this part of the world
has yet to be told. Yet, enough facts have been made public to

place the innate humanity and gallantry of the average Italian in their true perspective."[3] Tenenbaum probably based his observations on Léon Poliakov's book, "Harvest of Hate."[4] The historian today will regard such statements as oversimplifications which do not deserve to be included in history books.

The Italians divided their spoils of Yugoslavia's territory into a primary sector of occupation, Zone I, with civil administrative powers, which spelled outright annexation; and the so-called secondary military occupational sector Zone II. In Zone I, annexed directly by Italy, all military and civilian authorities were Italian. In Zone II, formally a part of the Independent State of Croatia, the civilian authorities were Croatian Ustashi. However, in Zone II the Italians were actually the rulers, permitting the Ustashi limited authority and power in administrative affairs. Il Duce was convinced in April, 1941 that Italy became richer because Dalmatia, Croatia proper, Slovenia, Bosnia and Herzegovina, Montenegro, and parts of Kosmet and Macedonia were occupied. Forty-eight hundred refugees fled into this Italian occupied territory; 2,000 into the annexation Zone I, 2,000 into occupation Zone II, and the rest into Montenegro and Kosmet. With the native Jewish population, the total numbered over 6,000.

The Italian occupants tolerated the Ustashi crimes which they could have prevented and were therefore responsible for them under Article 43 of the Hague Convention. The Italians contributed actively to the perpetration of the Ustashi crimes by making it impossible for the Jews to save themselves or by gathering and turning them over to the enemy.

In addition, the Italians tolerated the implementation of Pavelich's anti-Jewish laws, particularly in Dubrovnik where Jewish property was seized, and the Jews were sent to the concentration camps. The internment of all the Jews of Zone II was implemented by the order of the Italian command in November, 1942.[5]

The removal of Mussolini's Government and the attitude of Marshal Badoglio toward the interned Jews explains the supposedly contradictory saga of the Italians. Furthermore Mussolini was

---

[3] Wayne Publishers, New York, 1956, p. 304.

[4] Syracuse University Press, 1954, p. 158 and pp. 165-168.

[5] The Crimes of the Fascist Occupants and their Collaborators against Jews in Yugoslavia, Belgrade, 1957, pp. 22-24.

not sure whether to accede to German pressure and permit deportation. Often he would be persuaded by his commanders to delay the action.

Due to the procrastination on the part of the Italian Army and the new situation which arose after the collapse of Mussolini's government, some 2,500 Jews were still alive in Croatia by May of 1943. However the Germans, short in manpower, sent two White Russian divisions of Vlassov's army to Croatia. The Cossacks who fought poorly on the other fronts had a picnic in Croatia, where they ran riot and massacred Jews wherever they could find them. The tragic turn in the history of Yugoslav Jews started on April 6, 1941 when the aggressors attacked Yugoslavia. During more than four years—from April 10, 1941 until the early part of May, 1945—the tragic decimation of innocent men, women and children continued uninterruptedly.

4

Judges as
Commissioners

The letters and minutes included in this book are signed by two judges, who were appointed as commissioners of the Sephardic (over 9,000 persons) and Ashkenazic (over 1,000 persons) communities in Sarajevo. The judges were: Srechko Bujas and Branko Milakovich. They were made responsible for the registration of Jewish property and for keeping proper evidence of all Jews residing in Sarajevo. The Jews had to pay taxes and to register. Both judges were appointees of Ante Pavelich: Srechko Bujas, President of the District Court of Sarajevo, was appointed commissioner of the Sephardic Jewish Community on May 14, 1941, by the decree of the Poglavnik's Commission in Sarajevo, No. 227/41. Branko Milakovich, judge of the District Court of Sarajevo, was appointed commissioner of the Ashkenazic Jewish Community on May 31, 1941, by the decree of Poglavnik's Commission in Sarajevo, No. 1420/41.

Whether the judges knew in May, 1941, when they assumed the responsibility to serve as commissioners, that they would have to assist the authorities in "solving the Jewish problem" according to the "Ustashi manual" is not certain. It is reasonable to assume that their first and last concerns were for their own welfare and safety. However we must admit that the information acquired from them was often helpful. Furthermore the letters signed by them, addressed to the leaders of the Jewish Communities in Zagreb and Osijek, and their intervention, were tantamount to open criticism of the inhuman practice of the Ustashi regime. This, too, was an act of courage under the circumstances. Dr. M. Papo and Joseph Levi were most probably the true writers of these letters. Neverthe-less, the judges had to sign them before they could be mailed. They were "legally" responsible for correspondence written and signed by them.

The intervention of the judges resulted in a meeting between them and the authorities, who were in charge of sanitation and welfare in Sarajevo. While it is true that such a meeting was in the best interest of the whole population of Sarajevo, nevertheless their appeal for consideration was evident. It is true that their recommendations for achieving better conditions and treatment of the internees were ignored, and ultimately became totally mean-ingless.

It has not been proven that the judges played only a game, skillfully and cynically helping the Ustashi, by putting up a front and pacifying the victims. The language of compassion and an appeal to humane impulses was expressed in the letters, whether they were addressed to local or district authorities in Sarajevo, or the Ministry of Internal Affairs in Zagreb. It would have taken genuine heroes, individuals willing to sacrifice their lives, to defend the victims. The judges did not belong to this category. There was naïveté, which bordered on cynicism, when the commissioners appealed in a letter to the Jewish Community in Osijek, dated November 16, 1941, to obtain a list of Greek Orthodox (Serbian) internees in Jasenovac. It sounds as if the Jews had all necessary privileges and could perform the miracle of achieving results where the commissioners themselves had failed.

There is also proof that the commissioners, being jurists, believed that a state must have the authority, power and know how to decree orders and regulate rights of minorities even if they were considered "undesirable enemies and mediocre members of society." Srechko Bujas, the commissioner of the Sephardic community, intervened sometimes on behalf of arrested Jews, whenever members of their families informed him and asked for assistance. He visited jails, Ustashi offices and inquired about the fate of the arrested. Unable to obtain satisfactory information, he complained to the local Ustashi representatives, appointees of the Poglavnik: Hakija Hadjich and Bozhidar Bralo. Bralo was a Roman Catholic priest, who would permit the victims to become converts to Roman Catholicism and then pursue the practice of execution. Replying to Bujas' inquiry, Bralo cynically remarked that he was more concerned with saving the souls of the victims than with their physical survival and the guarantee of their lives. Some Jews in panic and despair embraced Roman Catholicism, hoping that this might end persecution. In the case of the Greek Orthodox people, conversion to Roman Catholicism was often equivalent to restoration of "full citizenship", and protection by the State. The question will have to remain unanswered whether the judges knew at the beginning, on April 10, 1941, to what all this would lead, and what course the "independent state of Croatia" would pursue.

We Jews had no knowledge in 1941 about the existence of crematoria; neither were the people in Yugoslavia aware of it. I was in contact with the Poles in Budapest from 1940. There was no indication in the oral reports and conversations which I was able to receive in 1940, and even in 1941, which would have hinted that extermination camps such as Auschwitz were in existence. To be in a concentration camp meant to us to lose freedom, to suffer and be deprived of one's family; but we were ignorant in spring 1941 of gas chambers or crematoria. I was Chief-Rabbi of the Jewish Community (Kehilah) in Osijek, capital of Slavonija, from 1937-1942. It became evident at the end of November, 1941 that the situation of the Jewish women and children interned in Sarajevo was desperate. The internees lacked adequate lodgings, food, clothing and medical help. The Commissioners of the Sephardic and Ashkenazic communities tried to alleviate the crisis by appealing for help to the Ustashi authorities as well as to the Jewish communities in Zagreb and Osijek.

The latter were doing their share by sending financial help, food and clothing. Furthermore Osijek and Zagreb supplied the infamous camp in Jasenovac with clothing, food, medicine and any

other articles requested by the camp's administration. A number
of scattered camps of former German, Austrian and other refugees
existed in Slatina, Chapljina, Brchko, which were deprived of the
most basic human necessities. The inmates managed to send
messages to us and cried for help and assistance.

In Sarajevo the victims were crowded in the damaged building
of "La Benevolencija" and smaller Jewish Temples, partly damaged as a result of bombings and partly demolished by the natives,
in the sections of the city known as Mejtasha and Charshija. In the
meantime an early and severe winter of 1941-42 was approaching.
The buildings mentioned were partly destroyed during the War.
They were without windows, water, electricity and medical care.
Food and bare necessities were scarcely available and the situation
became a living inferno. A transport of women and children from
these buildings directed to Loborgrad in January, 1942 was
returned to Sarajevo. The commander of the Loborgrad camp
refused to accept them. The victims were on the train without
food, water, etc., for eight days. Upon their return they were
placed in a school building, Marjin Court. The commissioners
Bujas and Milakovich complained to the Chief of Police with no
results, and ultimately appealed to the Great Zhupan (Prefect of
District Vrhbosnia) for help. When this too proved of no avail, the
commissioners, under the pressure of complaints by the native
population, who feared the spread of disease (typhus, diarrhea),
appealed to the Minister of Internal Affairs. The result was that
the Minister decreed the transfer of the Sarajevo women and
children to Djakovo and Stara Gradishka, where the last act of the
tragedy took place.

5

Tragedy's
Leading Characters

At the beginning of December, 1941 the Board of the Jewish Community in Osijek received the following order from the District Police in Osijek: "You will find within five days quarters for two thousand women and children who will be transferred from Sarajevo." The Jewish Community was informed that it would have to support, feed, clothe and care for the internees as well as to maintain the buildings. Upon receipt of this order, representatives of the Osijek Jewish Community searched throughout Slavonija for suitable accommodations. I happened to be in Djakovo (thirty kilometers from Osijek) officiating at a funeral. The mother and sister of my friend, Tibor Loebl, advised me that the former flour-mill building "Cereale," belonging to the estate of Bishop Alexander Akshamovich, was empty. I informed the acting President of the Board, Bela Friedman, about the "Cereale" in Djakovo.

I knew Bishop Akshamovich personally, having been Rabbi in Djakovo from 1932-1935. Akshamovich was interested in modern (conversational) Hebrew and I was his teacher for over two years. We used to take walks together in the park of his palatial residence. I was asked by Friedman to visit Akshamovich and to prepare the grounds. I anticipated a smooth and pleasant conversation with my former neighbor and pupil but was greatly disappointed. The Bishop did not hide his opposition to the idea of using his flour-mill as quarters for any internees. His diocese was now divided into parts as the result of the German-Yugoslav War in April, 1941. One half was under the political control of the Independent State of Croatia, while the other part was annexed by Horthy's Hungary. The Bishop encountered administrative difficulties as the result of the Hungarian occupation of Baranja, which was an integral part of his diocese. His personal uneasiness was partly due to his political, pro-Yugoslav orientation, prior to 1941. To say the least: he was not a persona grata in the eyes of the Ustashi Government in Zagreb.

Although the Djakovo office of the Bishop, supported by Archbishop Alois (Aloyze) Stepinac of Zagreb, opposed firmly the idea of a concentration camp within the confines of the Bishop's estate, the District Police in Osijek decreed that the flour-mill "Cereale" should be used as an official camp. It was convenient for the District Police in Osijek to have the camp in Djakovo because of its proximity. Furthermore there was no other place or building in all Slavonija that could be used for such a great number of women and children.

The Jewish Community in Osijek was charged with the administration of the camp, sharing this responsibility with the internees themselves. It was easier from our point of view to be effective and helpful in Djakovo than in Loborgrad, Jasenovac, Stara Gradishka, or any other place, distant from Osijek. Travel restrictions, supervision or even contact with internees presented great and insurmountable difficulties. The leaders of the Jewish Community in Zagreb saw, in the solution, a promising sign and preferred Djakovo to any other place in Slavonija, or any other part of Croatia proper, under the Ustashi. In the first place Osijek had hospital facilities; secondly it was almost on the borderline, dividing the Independent State of Croatia and Hungary. There were hopes connected with this imposed solution and responsi-

114929

bility. Contacts with friends among the Croats indicated that it was advantageous for the time being to stay in Slavonija rather than in Bosnia. Otherwise immediate deportation to Jasenovac or Auschwitz would have been the alternative.

The first and—following immediately—the second transport arrived in Djakovo with 1,830 Jewish women and children, and 50 Serbian girls. The head of the camp was named by the District Police, while the Jewish Community in Osijek took over the care of the internees, who were given the responsibility of maintaining supervision inside the camp.

The Jewish leaders in Osijek received a confidential report at the beginning of January, 1942 informing them that a large transport of Jewish and Serbian women and children arrived in Stara Gradishka. The condition of the internees was desperate. Food was immediately sent by the Osijek Community to alleviate the critical situation. Negotiations between the Jewish Communities in Zagreb and Osijek and the Ustashi authorities led to an agreement which was at first very promising. The district commander "permitted" the transfer of 1,200 Jewish and Serbian women and children from Stara Gradishka to Djakovo. The Jewish Communities in Osijek and Zagreb didn't know that the transferred internees were infected with typhus. The infection spread rapidly. After a short time 5-6 persons were dying every day. Then came diarrhea. The petition of the camp administration for erection of new latrines was rejected. Hunger reigned in the camp as the Ustashi seized all food sent by the Jewish Communities in Zagreb and Osijek. Rape and violation of women and girls were practiced in the camp almost daily. According to eyewitnesses 19 Jewish and 2 Serbian girls and young women were "selected to serve" in the office of the Ustashi elite. They were all killed in July, 1942 when the Djakovo camp was liquidated.

On March 29, 1942 the Ustashi from Jasenovac took over the camp in Djakovo. The District police was removed and the representatives of the Jewish Community of Osijek were forbidden entrance or contact with the internees or the camp. The Jewish leaders in Zagreb and Osijek were totally eliminated from any contact with the camp. In their despair, they appealed to Archbishop Stepinac and the Papal Nuncio, who tried to influence Pavelich to stop the persecution.

In June and July, 1942 the internees were transported to

Jasenovac where all of them were murdered in the Gradina. Five hundred and sixteen victims died in Djakovo and were buried at the Jewish cemetery. Several women saved their lives by being sent to the hospital in Osijek before the Ustashi took over the camp; a few escaped to Hungary. Jozo Matijevich, an Ustashi officer and his staff of highly experienced Jasenovac murderers, liquidated the Djakovo camp so that by the middle of July, 1942 there was not a single survivor.

An explanation of how these letters and minutes endured is in order. One of our secretaries employed by the Osijek Jewish Community was a young man, Valdimir (Vlado) Ginsberg, who resides in Israel. Dedicated, raised in the Zionist Youth movement, he was a highly reliable and courageous young man. Vlado typed, at my request, the correspondence between Zagreb, Sarajevo and Osijek in triplicate. The first copy was buried at Desatichina-ulica in Osijek, where the temporary quarters and offices of the Kehilah were located. We were ordered to evacuate and give up our own Community house, offices and premises at Radicheva-ulica. The second copy was entrusted to a woman of German origin, a resident of Osijek, who was related to a friend, Oskar Kishicky. The third copy was given to a Hungarian engineer-conductor who was in charge of the train commuting between Budapest and Osijek. He was reliable and lived in Budapest in the same apartment house in which my wife's parents resided. He was willing to serve as a courier, for which he was handsomely remunerated. He brought mail and food to us from Budapest and took our mail to our family and friends. The copy which he delivered to my wife's parents was found intact at the end of the War. It was hidden in a cellar among unimportant junk at Lazar-utca 14 in Budapest. The two other copies were destroyed. We brought the copy which was hidden in Budapest with us to the United States in 1948.

In 1966 the Sephardim of Sarajevo (and Bosnia) celebrated the 400th anniversary of organized Jewish communal life. Of the 10,500 Jews who lived in Sarajevo before World War II[6] only one thousand were present and participated in the festive celebrations. An old-new community which survived the inferno of Nazism,

---

[6] Zlochini Fashistichkih Okupatora i Njihovih Pomagacha Protiv Jevreja u Jugoslaviji, Belgrade, 1952.

Fascism and Utashism reviewed the history of its glory and tragedy.

Upon a famous bridge in Sarajevo, on the morning of June 28, 1914, a critical incident in world history took place. Archduke Francis Ferdinand, the heir-apparent to the Austro-Hungarian throne, was assassinated by a young Serbian nationalist, Gavrilo Princip. This tragedy in Sarajevo led to World War I, the war which supposedly was to end all wars. Historians analyzing the causes of World War I generally choose June 28, 1914 as the main reason for the beginning of hostilities leading to War. Although none of the Great Powers wanted a European war to the finish, nevertheless the undesired happened. With this realization World War I should have served as a lesson and reminder, a ghastly chapter of the past and a warning for the future.

6

Tito's
Partisans

The assassination of Archduke Francis Ferdinand triggered World War I, and today close to the bridge and the mosques the city's old synagogue is a memorial. The synagogue namely has been converted into a museum and shrine honoring the martyrs of Jewish Communities of Sarajevo. The lighting at the museum is dismal, the written explanations are only in Serbo-Croatian, and it is operated under the auspices of the state. The state is innocent of any aspect of local Jewish history as a heritage and part of the Jewish People. There is no Anti-Semitism, official or hidden, and Mosha Pijade, Tito's closest friend and advisor during the partisan years as well as post-war days, is revered throughout Yugoslavia as one of the "National Heroes" of the Anti-Fascist resistance, 1941-1945. Among those designated as national heroes were also Jews.

A walk through the synagogue-museum is similar to leafing through a sentimental old family album, starting with faded photos of the Sephardic merchants who led the Community. Sarajevo was a center of Hebrew culture, before living Hebrew became popular in Europe. Maccabbi, Hashomer Hatzair, a seminary for hahamim (spiritual leaders), a weekly newspaper in Serbo-Croatian (Jevrejski Glas), beautiful synagogues, all these were a part of pre-War Sarajevo. Today yellow stars, concentration camp garbs and other "insignia" displayed at the museum-memorial are reminders of Jasenovac, Auschwitz and other cremato ria. Nevertheless in Sarajevo's Museum of the Revolution, the fate of Yugoslavia's Jews, as Jews, is given prominent, respectful and dignified notice.

While it is true that Tito's pro-Arab policy is shared by both the Yugoslav Communist Party and the government, Yugoslavia's small Jewish community of approximately 6,500 is officially recognized and well treated. A cordial relationship exists between the Yugoslav Jews who settled in Israel and the remnant residing in Yugoslavia. The Yugoslav Jews participate freely in the activities of the World Jewish Congress. The attitude of Yugoslavia toward its surviving Jewish Community is favorable and distinguishes Tito's policy from other Communist nations such as the Soviet Union or Poland.

What was and is Josip Broz Tito's attitude toward the Jews during World War II, and toward Palestine as well as Israel, after the liberation and today? Here again it is only fair to make the distinction between the Jews of Yugoslavia and the Jewish State of Israel. As far as the Jewish State is concerned Tito's attitude has been influenced by two factors. First, Tito was one of the architects of the non-aligned nations responsible for the Third World as a force in world politics. Together with the late Gamal Nasser, President of Egypt, and Indira Gandhi, Prime Minister of India, he believes that a peaceful future for mankind depends upon the balance of power provided by "neutral nations" who are committed neither to the East or West. Second, millions of Moslems live in the republics of Bosnia-Herzegovina and Macedonia, which are a part of the Federative People's Republic of Yugoslavia. This alone would account for certain favorable political considerations as far as the Moslem world is concerned.

European partisans, whether Communist oriented or not, did not use the same methods in their fight against the invaders. They differed in their political, ideological and often strategic methods and tactics. One must remember that the Yugoslav Partisan movement came into existence in July, 1941. The internment of the Jews of Yugoslavia in camps took place in 1941 at a time when the partisan movement was about to be organized and activated. It is indeed a moot question whether Tito's Partisans could have been more helpful to the oppressed Jews in their struggle for survival. It is easy to engage in hindsight strategy. The partisans had to meet unexpected situations. They fought a powerful and well-organized enemy. There were and are critics who claim that Tito forbade in 1941 the acceptance of young Jews into the ranks of the partisans. Research into and first hand knowledge of the resistance in Yugoslavia indicate that the movement was basically anti-Fascist and therefore welcomed all fighters. Many young Jews served with the partisans, and a great number of them fell in the conflict.

Hashomer Hatzair members were among the first known resistance fighters who attacked a German truck in Belgrade and the Italian officers' club in Cetinje, capital of Montenegro. On July 26, 1941 Hayim Almoslino, 17 years old, set on fire a German motorcycle. Thereupon the German Police for Jews in Belgrade issued an order that all Jews were to assemble the next day, July 27th, 1941 at Tashmajdan. The terror was dreadful; 1,200 Jews reported or were brought in. The Germans divided them according to their professions and every tenth individual was declared a hostage. The hostages were taken to Jajinci and executed on July 29th, 1941. Almoslino's bravado was an act by a desperate young man expressing condemnation, disgust and opposition to what was happening. The partisans could have taken advantage of it and could have recruited boys like him into their ranks. Why they did not do so remains an unanswered question. In August, 1941 all Jewish men in Serbia were in concentration camps and by December, 1941 all Jewish women found the same destiny. Tito's forces were driven back in November, 1941 and compelled to retreat from Serbia into the mountains of Bosnia and Montenegro. After their defeat of November, 1941 only small units remained in Serbia. These partisan units were capable of acts of sabotage but could not help the doomed Jews because they were too small in number and too poorly armed to be effective against the larger German forces.

During the summer of 1941 Croatian Jews found themselves in a similar situation. First, men were taken to concentration camps and soon women were sent there as well. A highly demoralized and disorganized situation existed. Yugoslavia was divided into German, Italian, Hungarian occupation zones and the so-called "Independent State of Croatia." This made coordination, or even exchange of information, among Yugoslav Jewish Communities impossible! Yugoslavia reminded one in spring of 1941 of a country that was hit by a hurricane. Families were separated, lines of communication interrupted, law and order replaced by confusion and chaos. The Germans used the following method: In most cities the local "Volksbund" had prepared a list of Jewish public workers, leaders of Jewish institutions and agencies. Religious funtionaries were among the first to be arrested, together with leading intellectuals, industrialists and financiers.

Two points should be made to explain why the number of Jews among the partisans was not greater, although there were many Jews among them. First there were no contacts between Tito's partisans and the Jews at the beginning of the German occupation of Yugoslavia, although such contacts could have been established. The reason is simple. Most Jews did not know where to go or how to seek the partisans out. Even if they wanted to do so, and this was almost impossible, they would have needed help from the outside. On the other hand the partisans, small in numbers in spring 1941, were too busy getting started and organized. They made no attempts to recruit fighters from among the Jews. It seems that guerrilla movements were not concerned with oppressed Jews outside of their ranks, regardless of whether or not these guerrillas were Communist oriented and trained. A number of partisan units were operating in Serbia and elsewhere under Communist command. They consisted of small groups of determined men and women, but mostly party members, who, at a word from party headquarters, had taken to the woods and forests. Early in July, 1941 news began to reach Belgrade of their achievements; of ambushed German convoys and of surprise attacks upon enemy outposts and units.

In Slavonija, a part of Croatia proper, attempts were made by individual Jews to establish contacts with Tito's partisans. Three Jewish women in Osijek joined a partisan cell in the summer, 1941. They were: Anica Adler, Stephanie Nagy and Luci Gutman. The Ustashi discovered the cell, arrested the leader and promised him clemency provided he would give them the names of the other members. To save his own life the cell leader, who was an Aryan, betrayed the Jewish women and gave their names to the prosecutor. The women were tried and executed by the Ustashi in the jail court of Osijek in early autumn, 1941.

Marsh, the Ustashi investigator, occupied half of the large, two-story house owned by Nagy. He permitted Stephanie's husband to observe shiva (seven days of mourning) and to hold

services in his presence. "You pray in Hebrew?" he asked me.
"Yes," I replied, "and I will bring along two copies of our
prayerbook; one copy with a Serbo-Croatian and the second with
a German translation." Marsh found the suggestion to his liking.
He sat during the services holding the prayerbook in his hand and
reading the translation. At the end of the Shiva, Marsh asked Nagy
in my presence to give him Stephanie's fur coats and other
belongings which he wanted for his mother and girl friend. Nagy
agreed willingly.

Marsh turned to me and added: "We could have indicted you as
well. You were seen frequently according to our information with
two of the executed women." "Well," I replied, "suppose you
were seen with your priest recently? Does this imply that you
discussed politics with him? You could have enjoyed simply
talking or listening to him. People usually want to see their pastors
when they have questions pertaining to religious matters." "One
thing more," Marsh added, "the local German newspaper wrote
about you stating that while your parishioners are busy contacting
partisans, you are walking daily in the streets of Osijek with a
smiling face as if we were living in 1940." "I read the article, Mr.
Marsh," I answered, "but believe me I have no reason whatsoever
to be smiling nowadays." "Take the hint for what it is worth," he
said, concluding our conversation. I lived with and remembered
the hint every day and every hour of the day for the next six
months.

It must be stated that the Jews had no clear conception of what
awaited them at the hands of the Germans. The Nazi were masters
in spreading and fostering illusions among their victims. Furthermore, the partisans operated most of the time far away from the
areas of Jewish internments and it was almost impossible to
contact or join them. It should be pointed out that among the
partisans were also men who did not understand the difficulty and
peculiarity of the Jewish situation. However they did not represent the official views of the partisan leadership or the liberation
movement as such.

Mosha Pijade described[7] the attitude of the Soviet Union which
made many excuses and refused to dispatch its parachutists to the
partisans. Tito personally reassured Stalin that the parachutists

[7] About the Legend that the Yugoslav Uprising owed Its Existence to Soviet
Assistance, London, 1950.

would be completely protected while on liberated Yugoslav soil. Tito and the Yugoslav Communists never forgot or forgave Stalin and the Soviets for not sending as much as a hand grenade during these years of despair and struggle. Tito's and Pijade's books contain many biting remarks concerning this refusal of help.

Objection and criticism were raised regarding young Jews who were liberated from camps and thrown into the front lines without any previous training or efficient equipment. As a result such units were wiped out and slaughtered by superior German soldiers and arms. It has been pointed out that guerilla warfare was marked by unexpected, dangerous, quick decisions and moves. Fighters were often thrown into battles and lost their lives because there was no chance for survival.[8] When this happened the reason for this kind of military operation might have been that there was no other choice. Professional officers, on all fronts, made similar decisions in order to give the embattled units a moment of relief and support.

David Alkalai, a man of integrity and eminence as a Jewish leader, writes: "I do not know of a single instance of the loss of an entire Jewish group in battle. Not one of the partisans who returned from the war has claimed that the attitude toward the Jewish fighters differed in any way from that toward any others."[9] Historians who have researched the predicament of the Jews at Bor feel that Alkalai exaggerates when he defends the partisans and their indifference. The laborers-inmates of the Bor mines were not only Hungarian but also Yugoslav Jews. Tito's partisans had a moral obligation and responsibility to help their own compatriots. They knew that Bachka and Baranja Jewish citizens were in the Bor forced labor camp. The fact that they were outnumbered by other (Hungarian) Jews does not change the basic concept of responsibility and "unity of all Yugoslavs: Serbs, Croats, Slovenes, Montenegrins, Moslems and others regardless of race and religion." This is the way Tito spoke and declared his policy at Bihach in 1942 while addressing the representatives of Yugoslavia who supported him.[10]

The camp at Bor, Northern Serbia, was a copper mine where Hungarian Jews (munkaszolgálatos) chiefly worked as forced

---

[8] Tito the Man who defied Hitler and Stalin, Ballantine Books, New York, 1957.

[9] "Tito's Record Toward the Jews," Jewish Frontier, February, 1953.

[10] Josip Broz Tito, Borba za Oslobodjenje Jugoslavije, Belgrade, 1947, p. 107.

laborers. In 1941 the Hungarian Government under László Bárdossy introduced a law concerning deportation of "foreign Jews," and regulations regarding "stateless" residents who were to be placed in concentration camps. The Anti-Jewish legislation also introduced special "forced labor" cadres. The member of the forced labor units wore a Hungarian military cap, semi-military shoes, but civilian clothing. He also wore a yellow badge on the right arm. Converts to Christianity wore a white badge instead of a yellow. In February, 1943 the Germans asked the Hungarian Government to send 10,000 Jewish men of the "forced labor" group to work in the copper mines at Bor. After months of negotiations and delay the Hungarians yielded and escorted 10,000 Jews to Bor. Tito's partisans were accused of opposing military action aimed at liberating this contingent of Hungarian and Yugoslav Jews in the copper mines of Bor. It was not until 1944 that the partisans attacked Bor and liberated the surviving Hungarian Jews. The majority of the 10,000 internees had been murdered by the Nazis and Hungarians by the time they retreated. The inmates could have been liberated sooner if the partisans would have energetically concentrated on the liberation of Bor. Bor and the tragedy of the Hungarian "forced labor" units is a part of a two volume documentary history, published in Hungarian. The editor justifiably used the following slogan as the title of the book: "They Stood Unarmed on the Minefields."[11]

The Germans began evacuating Bor in the middle of September, 1944 as the Red Army was approaching. The first column of 3,600 Jewish workers, escorted by Hungarian guards, started the retreat on September 17, 1944. Among the members of this group were nearly all the Jews from Bachka and Baranja, formerly Yugoslavian territory. They were bilingual, spoke Serbo-Croatian and Hungarian, and reached the infamous Belgrade Sajmishte camp on September 25th. From here they were taken from the Sajmishte camp via Hungarian—former Yugoslavian—cities to various concentration camps in Germany. Most of them were transferred to Fossenburg and Buchenwald. They found the same fate here as did other Jews interned in these camps. Of 5,000-6,000 retreating Jews who worked in Bor, only 9 survived. The copper mine at Bor, its victims and Tito's partisans are closely

[11] Elek Karsai, Fegyvertelen Áltak az Aknamerzökön, Budapest, 1962. Nahman Blumenthal, The Plight of Jewish Partisans, Yad Vashem Bulletin, April, 1957.

linked. The camp was located on Yugoslav territory. Some of its inmates were Yugoslav citizens, and the partisans operated successfully in northern Serbia.

Objectivity and historicity require that we mention that Tito's partisans liberated the Jewish concentration camps in the Italian zone of occupation and transferred their inmates to the free territory under Partisan Administration. Hinko Gottlieb was a Zagreb lawyer, former editor of "Omanut" magazine, a writer, and a community leader and he was one of the people liberated in the Italian zone. Gottlieb described the behavior of the partisans in a series of sketches and stories in the Hebrew press of Israel and praised the partisans for their deeds of courage, kindness and understanding.

The infamous concentration camp Crveni Krst, near Nish, came into existence about the middle of October, 1941 and was under the direction of the Gestapo. Among the inmates were men, women and small children, as well as the very old and sick. When the partisans attacked Nish at the end of 1941 and liberated the camp, they called upon the Jews to follow them. Unfortunately the liberation lasted only a few hours before the partisans were forced to retreat. Only a small number of the inmates followed the partisans' call. These were principally single people who had no family ties to the camp. Those who hesitated because they did not want to leave the old and sick, paid a high price for their loyalty. More than one thousand inmates remained in camp and were exterminated by the Germans a few days later. The Crveni Krst camp existed through 1942-1943 with new inmates brought in from East and West Serbia. The last Jewish inmate of the camp was murdered in November, 1943.

Tito's attitude toward Jewish immigration to Palestine from 1945-1948 and to Israel after the establishment of the State was benevolent. Yugoslavia was a thoroughfare for immigrants en route to Palestine from camps or central European countries. The small Adriatic ports became centers for Hagganah vessels which transported "repatriates" with Greek and Italian names and papers. The Yugoslav authorities, from the border guards to the secret police, knew about the illegal immigration. They did not question the right of the Jewish people to fight for their independence and were helpful in many ways during those difficult and critical days. Tito's Government broke off diplomatic relations with Israel after

June, 1967. Some newspapermen claim that Tito and Yugoslavia's leaders consider the 1967 diplomatic incident a mistake and are waiting for a new opportunity to correct the situation and to resume diplomatic relations.

Zionism was very popular in pre-War Yugoslavia, among the young in particular. The Hashomer Hatzair movement of Yugoslavia gave Israel's Army the last two Chiefs of Staff, Hayim Bar Lev and David (Dado) Eleazar. Israel's eighth and ninth Chiefs of Staff bring honor to their comrades-in-arms who fell in Yugoslavia while surrounded by cruel enemies, the German Army, the Ustashi, the Volksbund, and a highly demoralized society. After 1945 nothing was done to reorganize the Zionist movement. The Yugoslav Jews, among them Zionists, were wise in making concessions and in avoiding a Communist-Zionism controversy which led to arrests, persecution and liquidation of Zionist press and institutions in other satellite countries such as Hungary, Poland, Rumania, Bulgaria and Czechoslovakia. The Jews of Yugoslavia and their leaders were divided in two groups. The larger group wanted to emigrate to Israel. Its leaders felt that it was more practical not to engage in an ideological confrontation with the Communist Party, which kept a vigilant eye on all dissenters and their activities. The smaller group and its leaders decided to remain in Yugoslavia and to adhere to the political and social principles of an emerging, new society. They were entitled to build their future as they saw fit. Sixty percent went to Israel and forty percent remained in Yugoslavia. The Jews are represented in all walks of life. They are employed by the Government in various enterprises or serve directly in all kinds of governmental agencies. There are even signs of search for Jewish identity among the members of this small remnant of Yugoslavia's Jews. They have no temples or religious functionaries and invite outsiders to conduct High Holy Day services in the larger communities. Attempts are being made to help the young people to attend Jewish summer camps, where Jewish identity and heritage can be cultivated. It is not being done during the school year and the parents are not able to do it, because they lack knowledge. Most of the Yugoslav Jews are graduates of concentration camps and forests.

7

The

"Judenraete"

There were no Judenraete (Jewish Councils) in Yugoslavia in the usual sense of the word. Congregations merged wherever there were two in one town; such as orthodox and liberal (neolog), Ashkenazic and Sephardic, downtown and uptown. The boards of Jewish Communities "played the game" cautiously, stalling for time and helping the old, sick and the children, whom they did not want to abandon. The "plan" was based on the principle of "HAYEY SHAA," meaning "life for an hour," or survive today, and try again tomorrow. The term "plan" is being used as an euphemism. The Jewish communities did not become tools in the hands of their oppressors. Neither did they serve the oppressors by providing lists or information.

There was no Jewish Police in the camps or transition centers in either Croatia or Yugoslavia. The Jewish Police in the European ghettos were bitterly hated. And, indeed, they wrote a black page in the book of holocaust history. It is true that Jewish leaders in Croatia were often in the precarious position of negotiating with the killers. They did it, however, with dignity and a deep sense of responsibility. Dedicated, courageous and devoted men directed survival attempts by helping those who might have decided to cross the border into Hungary or Italy or to obtain a visa to a neutral country. The leaders waited patiently for the right moment for themselves, hoping to escape deportation.

The difference, for example, between Zagreb and Budapest, Osijek and Amsterdam, or Belgrade and Salonica is best described as follows: In Budapest the Judenrat existed for less than 9 months, the last year of the War. This situation prevented the Budapest Judenrat from becoming an instrument in the hands of the oppressors although it moved in that direction. Furthermore the neutrals representing Sweden, Switzerland, Spain, Portugal and the Vatican were active since summer, 1944 encouraging the survival of the Jews and promoting hope among them. It is almost certain that the Judenrat in Budapest would have played a tragic role in the deportation scheme would it have been in existence for longer than 9 months. The Jewish communities in Salonica and Amsterdam are very sad examples of being misled rather than led in time of crisis.[12] On the other hand, Zagreb's Jewish Community leaders were exposed to pressure beginning in April, 1941. The same is true of Osijek. They met the challenge. Many died because of their courage and loyalty. Among them were those who stubbornly believed that it was possible to survive, although life became very difficult and dehumanized. Dr. Shalom Freiberger, the last Rabbi of Zagreb, was deported to Auschwitz, in May, 1943, despite assurances by Archbishop Stepinac, who repeatedly told him to remain in Zagreb. The Archbishop was misled by the Ustashi, who promised him that they would not bother the only remaining Rabbi of Croatia.

The Jews of Osijek were trapped when the Ustashi offered them the village of Tenje, near Osijek. They were told they could build their own settlement there which would serve as their own community until the end of the War. The Ustashi liquidated the settlement after a few months and deported all Jews in Tenje to

---

[12] J. Presser, The Destruction of the Dutch Jews, New York, 1969–Jewish Frontier, August, 1953.

Auschwitz, Jasenovac and Loborgrad. This included not only the Jews from Osijek but also those from the neighboring towns. The tragedy of the Tenje settlement proved that even intelligent and courageous people were naive enough to trust hangmen and to believe their sincerity. So were betrayed Jewish citizens, who trusted the Ustashi murderers.

Croatian Jews, small in numbers, were unprepared to meet the savagery of the Ustashi, although its leaders understood the nature of the War and Nazism much better than the men in charge of Yugoslavia's affairs. Still they could not imagine that a complete "extermination plan" was prepared. Even the most pessimistic of the leaders of Yugoslavia's Jewry could not have foreseen Jasenovac and Shabats. Yugoslav anti-Semitism hardly existed before 1941, although the so-called Koroshets laws of 1940 forbade the exercise of some professions by the Jews and limited their rights to education. The Yugoslav rulers believed that by cooperating with Fascism the country could avoid occupation and stay out of the War.

While Roosevelt's America refused to admit Jewish refugees, and the British closed the doors to Palestine, even Tenje looked promising, as a temporary solution.

8

The Croatian
Theresienstadt

Tenje was not another Terezin (Theresienstadt) although it looked promising to the Jewish community of Osijek. After all, Tenje, like Terezin, was not a concentration camp in the ordinary sense of the word. It was supposed to become a town inhabited by Jews and governed by them; a settlement in which every manner of work was to be done by Jewish hands. What more could the Jews expect, the Ustashi asked. The Ustashi—faithful disciples of the Nazis-Fascists—trapped their victims by spreading rumors that the representatives of the International Red Cross would inspect the settlement and provide the Jews of Tenje with international protection in accordance with The Hague and Geneva conventions. It is easy to understand that a drowning man will cling to a straw. The Jews of Osijek and its environs were under the spell of an illusion.

The Ustashi authorities did not hesitate to go through a "legal" procedure, which proved to be a farce. An agreement was included in the minutes which promised the Osijek Jewish Community protection of life and property once they settled in Tenje. The agreement signed by Jews and Ustashi authorities was an official, legal document. The Ustashi hinted that they might be willing to permit the transfer of small children to a neutral country under the supervision of the International Red Cross. Seven hundred children were among the three thousand Jews, many of them from Sarajevo, who were "rescued" in 1941 and sent to Osijek, where Jewish families adopted them lovingly. Only people who experienced during 1939-45 what "hayey shaa" (life for an hour) meant will understand the predicament of parents, relatives and neighbors, who transferred a child from one area where the volcano already had erupted to a less dangerous place, hoping that the child would survive. Were those people responsible for transferring children "pious fools" in the sense of a rabbinic dictum? According to the Rabbis a pious fool is one, "who sees a child struggling in the water, and says, 'when I have taken off my phylacteries, I will go and save him,' and while he does so, the child breathes his last."[13] The truth is that no one can judge people and situations from hindsight. Unfortunately this was done by historians, philosophers and psychiatrists with a great deal of perverted zeal.

The author was approached as early as December, 1940 by the Polish Government-in-exile, Budapest Branch, to join them as a representative of the Jews. The Poles-in-exile were very anxious to prove their concern for the Jews in Poland and elsewhere. They wanted to impress the Allies in the West. A Jew active in the Budapest Branch would serve this purpose. I refused twice to do so and explained my reason. It was my moral duty to be with my congregation. By January, 1942 the Poles came for the third time and brought a letter from Professor Lercher, my history teacher at the Gymnasium in Tarnopol. This time I asked the messengers to come back in a month or two to which one of them replied: "You are naive, in a month no Jew will be left in Osijek." He explained the German methods of evacuation and transfer from one place to another. I shared this information with confidants of mine, Bela

[13] A Rabbinic Anthology, Meridian Books, Cleveland and New York, 1960, p. 487 (1385).

Friedman, President of the Osijek community; Dr. Leon Margulies, my wife's uncle; and Dr. Ljudevit Rosenberg, a prominent lawyer. The conference lasted only a few minutes. We came to the following conclusion: Every individual, or family, may look for an escape before Tenje becomes a reality if he has an opportunity. This was nothing new because we pursued this policy of helping people to escape to Italy or Hungary from summer, 1941. Many escaped while others were caught in their attempt and returned to the Ustashi. Dr. Freiberger had sensed the danger of trusting the Ustashi, who promised Archbishop Stepinac that he, as the Rabbi of Zagreb, and the remnant of the Jewish Community would be protected. This included the old, the sick, the children and specially trained professionals. On a piece of a newspaper which Dr. Freiberger's messenger brought to us two Hebrew words were written: B'RAH L'HA (Flee at once). The messenger, a trusted man, and a Seventh Day Adventist Minister, explained: Freiberger felt that at least one Rabbi should be active outside of Croatia in order to contact the International Red Cross, the Vatican, neutrals and of course our own people. He also urged Dr. Simon Ungar, the retired Chief-Rabbi of Osijek to try to escape into Hungary, where he had relatives and friends.

This was a time of anxiety and despair and we had not heard from the Poles for some time after our December, 1941 meeting. My wife and I had given up hope of seeing them again. To our great surprise the Poles arrived at the right moment. We were fortunate to be contacted at the twelfth hour by these Polish underground messengers from Budapest. In the chaos which prevailed, they suggested crossing the river Drava (Drau), the borderline between Croatia and Hungary. To cross the Drava in February was perilous. The ice began melting in the middle of the river and the darkness of the night was an added danger confronting us. However, we succeeded and an automobile was waiting for us at the other bank of the Drava. When we arrived in Budapest, my wife had to be admitted immediately to a hospital inasmuch as she had a 105° temperature. The next day I met with Elizabeth Kurz, at Andrássy ut 2, who introduced me to the leaders of the Vaada Ezra V'hatzalah (Rescue Council). The next day I met the two men who were most active in the Hungarian underground. They were the controversial Dr. Rezso Kastner and his closest friend, Joel Brand.

Refusal to accept Tenje would have led to immediate deportation. In this desperate situation, with no hope of help from
anybody, the Jews of Osijek accepted Tenje, which they built
using their own hands and means. The Jews were convinced that
there was no alternative. Ultimately they were deported to
Jasenovac and Auschwitz on August 15, 18 and 22, 1942. Of the
3,000 Jews deported in August, 1942 only ten persons returned
after the War.

After 1945, trials were held against Rabbis who served in
Vienna, Budapest and Salonica. In Vienna and Salonica the Rabbis
became tools of the Gestapo.[14] In Budapest one Rabbi cooperated with Szálasi's Minister of Propaganda and the Arrow-Cross
Party.[15] Rabbis and religious functionaries in Yugoslavia were
fortunate not to be directly involved in contacts or negotiations
with the executioners.

In Osijek, my predecessor of blessed memory, Simon Ungar and
I immediately after Passover, 1941 visited the following clergymen, representing all religio-ethnic groups, and asked them for
help. We met with Senior Walter of the Lutheran Evangelical
Church who was popular among the local Germans, the Monsignor, who was influential among the Croats, the Pastor of the
Calvinistic Church, which served the Hungarians. The Greek
Orthodox were also persecuted by the Ustashi and therefore
could be of no help. The Seventh Day Adventist Minister came to
us and graciously offered his aid. They all were helpful in one way
or another. Senior Walter, whose son served as chaplain in the
German Army said to me on one occasion that should the German
people find themselves in jeopardy and facing danger, then he
would pray to God like Moses, "erase me from the book which
You have written." I must admit that his statement made an
impression on me. We continued our conversation and parted as
friends. One day I was leaving his house after a lengthy conversation when he reassured me stating: "Whenever you will be in
danger I will do my utmost to help you, and I hope that you will
reciprocate should I need your assistance." He kept his promise on
two very critical occasions. Once he intervened when the local

[14] Drs. Benjamin Mumerlstein and Zvi Korez.

[15] Dr. Bela Berend (Presser).

Volksbund arrested me for no reason whatsoever. The second time, an SS man was attacked and the easiest thing was to detain me as a hostage. His intervention led to my release on both occasions. In spring, 1946 I recognized Senior Walter in Munich as he was walking in front of a hotel. He left Osijek with the retreating German Army and was a refugee in West Germany. I asked him whether he needed help. Senior Walter was unemployed, and I was very glad to provide him with a considerable sum of money mindful of his assistance in the critical years of 1941-1942.

Rabbis in Croatia performed their duties and left the negotiations with the Ustashi to the administrative arm of the congregation. The Rabbis' influence was used in approaching clergy. Rabbi Freiberger was the liaison between the Jews, Archbishop Stepinac and the Vatican. He succeeded in organizing a group of children who were sent to Palestine in winter 1943, via Budapest. Among them was his only son Reuben. Reuben Freiberger became a gifted musician and changed his name to Jaron. He was eleven years old when he came to the Kibbutz Shaar Haamakim in Palestine in 1943. He found relatives in the Kibbutz, who adopted him and assumed the responsibility for his well being. The Kibbutz sent him to Tel Aviv to study music in a conservatorium. He married at the age of twenty-four. Young, gifted, lively and enthusiastic Reuben was killed three months later, on November 3, 1956, at the front, during the Sinai campaign. Archbishop Stepinac and the Papal Nuncio were very helpful in getting permission from the Ustashi government so that this group of Jewish children could leave Zagreb legally. A great majority of the rabbis perished. Those who survived were simply fortunate, not clever! Sushak must be mentioned because of its important role and the tragic end of its Rabbi. The Italian commander-administrator of Sushak was informed by Rabbi Deutch of the humanitarian work he was performing among refugees, who came from other parts of Croatia, to seek refuge under Italian occupation. Genoveso approved the Rabbi's activity and trapped Rabbi Deutch, promising him to decentralize the ever growing number of Croatian and other refugees in Sushak. He got the list with the names of the refugees, from Rabbi Deutch. As a result, these refugees were arrested and returned to Croatian territory which was under the Ustashi administration. The Rabbi, however, was sent to Ferramonte camp. Suffering from depression as a result of Genoveso's betrayal and action, Rabbi Deutch showed signs of mental disorder. He was transferred to a mental institution in Nucera Inferiore, Italy, where he passed away. So ended tragically a naive, but innocent man. His death adds another chapter to the volume of history which so many rightfully describe as "man's inhumanity to man."

It is well to remember, the Yugoslav Jews were not the only ones whose unpreparedness of the German onslaught in April 1941 made them vulnerable. The Soviets, for instance, described the shock experienced by their citizens in June 1941 when they realized that the behavior of the Germans in the occupied territory bordered on barbarism. They could not, at first, believe the news about German atrocities, mass killing of soldiers as well as civilians. They remembered what Stalin told Emil Ludwig in his famous interview that the Germans were reliable, sober and solid people. It took months to convince the Soviet citizens that their image of the civilized and orderly German was based on a misconception.

The Croatian Jews were squeezed in between the onslaught of the Ustashi, who were supervised by the Germans, and the Italian Fascists, who were constantly reminded by the Nazis of their racial duty as allies. This is worth remembering when we study the Holocaust and the survival of Jews; the chances for survival in Yugoslavia were very slim.

9

The Mufti
of Jerusalem

What makes Destruction and Survival of Sarajevo's Jews so unique is the fact that the former Mufti of Jerusalem, Hadj Amin El Husseini was a frequent guest in Zagreb. He was the chief organizer of the S.S. division of Moslems in Bosnia. The division was named "Handjar"–"Sword." The Mufti supervised the extermination of Balkan Sephardic communities, particularly those of Yugoslavia, from his headquarters in Berlin and Zagreb. The Moslems residing in Bosnia-Herzegovina and Macedonia were his most faithful followers. As late as April 22, 1944 the Handjar division was active in liquidating the remaining hidden Jews in Tuzla, Srebrenik and Duboshnica. The leader of one S.S. Handjar group was a Volksdeutcher. A photo shows the official Arab leader of Palestine surrounded by Ustashi members of the Pavelich government.

After the unconditional surrender of Germany in May, 1945, the Grand Mufti of Jerusalem, an honored guest and ally in Germany since early November, 1941 found his way safely to Cairo where he now resides. He watched jealously and organized European Moslems into military units. The Mufti intrigued among leading European politicians so that no Jew be left alive on the European continent. Heinrich Himmler complimented the Grand Mufti on his blue eyes, on one occasion, formal proof of his Nordic descent. The two leaders met at a tea given in honor of the Mufti by Himmler. A small circle of high-ranking S.S. officers were present. The conversation was very animated and even the Turks were highly praised as compared with "Judaized Christianity." Two flags, the Swastika and the Crescent were flown together to symbolize friendship between two diametrically different concepts and ideas. It seems that corruption and hypocrisy have no boundaries.

Paul Joseph Goebbels wrote in his Diaries[16] on January 30, 1942: "It is interesting to observe what importance the clever exploitation of religion can assume. The Tartars at first had a none-too-gratifying attidude toward the German Wehrmacht. But they changed about completely when permitted to sing their religious chants from the tops of the minarets. Their change of attitude went so far that Tartar auxiliary companies which fought actively against the Bolsheviks could be formed. Our efforts were supported by our propaganda companies who distributed a picture showing the Grand Mufti of Jerusalem visiting the Fuehrer. That was extremely successful." Goebbels ridiculed the Moslems, calling them Tartars, but Hitler nevertheless graciously received their spiritual leader, the Mufti of Jerusalem, on December 8, 1941.

It is interesting to note that the same Haj Amin el Hussein, who visited Germany early in November, 1941, then went to Italy for about a month, and returned permanently to Berlin, where he established his headquarters. When he wanted to go to London in August, 1946 as a member of the Arab delegation, the British Government, in spite of their willingness to cater to the Arabs as much as possible, refused permission because of the Mufti's pro-Axis activities during 1941-5.

The Germans played the "game" shrewdly. Goebbels and Himmler had little admiration for non-Aryans. Anyone, including the Tartars, was good and acceptable as long as he served their purpose. Race theory and racial purity could be "adjusted," as in the case of the Croatian leaders, who had Jewish wives and whose children were half Jewish, according to the race-religion of Aryan salvation and the ideal of the Nordic man. As long as the dream of achieving a Pan-German world conquest was not fulfilled, shaking hands and drinking tea with Tartars was morally justified. After all, the Mufti could help to organize badly needed divisions and manpower. Goebbels was an educated man who held a Doctor of Philosophy degree. All his articles carried the full title, Reich-

[16] Eagle Book Edition, New York, 1948, p. 73.

minister Dr. Goebbels. His use of the term "Tartar" was not a
Freudian slip. It really meant an irritating, violent, intractable
person. In any case, it was not a compliment. Goebbels confined
his inner feelings to paper rather than to the public. After all his
"Diaries" were his private possession.

The Mufti is among the "righteous untouchables" who were not
tried and escaped punishment. He had "powerful friends" who
saw to it that his return was safe-guarded and pleasant. He was not
the only untouchable, who should have been tried. Both sides, in
the camp of the Allies, practiced the same policy of prosecuting
some of the guilty War criminals and of protecting others who
could be useful eventually. Criminals such as A. Pavelich and E.
Kavaternik found refuge in Argentina.

Charles R. Allen, Jr. described the futile attempts to bring A.
Artukovich to trial.[17] His atrocities against Serbs and Jews, when
he served as Minister of Interior of the Independent State of
Croatia, have been proven and documented. The "Eichmann of
Croatia" lives comfortably in Long Beach, California, where his
rich family resides. U.S. Commissioner Theodore Hoche ignored
the evidence presented by the Yugoslav Government at the
"hearing" held in Los Angeles and denied the application for
extradition.

A private bill which granted Artukovich permanent residence in
the United States and, thereby, obviated any chance of extradition, was introduced by U.S. Congressman, James B. Utt. From
time to time prominent journalists (such as the late Drew Pear-
son), magazines, such as Newsweek,[18] ask the same question again
and again. How is it possible? What are the forces behind
Artukovich which provide him this kind of protection? The Mufti
of Jerusalem and Artukovich belong to the category of "hypocrisy
and flagrant dishonesty" on the stage of international politics.
This is difficult to accept.

More than fifty million people perished as the result of World
War II, but the cynical doctrines of Machiavelli are still regarded
and practiced as the gospel of our age. What Niccolo Machiavelli
expressed in his celebrated treatise "The Prince" almost five
centuries ago, is presently practiced in Washington, Moscow, Paris,
London and many other capitals of the world.

[17] Jewish Currents, New York, March, 1963.

[18] July 7, 1958, p. 27.

10

Ray of Hope

Yugoslav Jews were in a better position after the end of the war than their fellow Jews in other countries. The suffering of Jewish communities in Europe continued long after May, 1945. The slow and painful process of convalescence, the laborious attempts of rebuilding shattered lives were supported by Tito's government. The Yugoslav-Jewish community could build life anew in an environment which was conducive. Tito's government was helpful and did not permit any kind of hostility towards its Jewish citizens. They were treated justly. Even in a democratic Holland Jewish survivors were treated with dislike, scorn and suspicion. The situation in Poland was much worse. Polish students organized a daylight pogrom in July 1946, barely a year after the end of the War.

There was no "post-war attitude" towards Jewish citizens in Yugoslavia. It is true that each individual was forced to build up his entire life anew. But he did not feel unwelcomed. Those who returned with the partisans as well as those who survived in Italy, Hungary or in hiding experienced mental tensions and grief about their families, but they were no strangers in their homeland. These were positive and encouraging signs. They indicated the emergence of a new Jewish community in Yugoslavia. It was less colorful perhaps, though hardly less many-sided. We have spoken of a new Jewish community. Can we really call it that? After all sixty percent left for Israel. It would be justified to speak of a group.[19] A group pieced together after May 1945, from a host of fragments.

The synagogues had been desecrated and destroyed during the occupation. They have not been rebuilt. The religio-cultural life which once centered around the synagogue does not exist anymore. On the other hand Jewish cemeteries desecrated are being looked after in an admirable way and are well kept. There are no rabbis, cantors or teachers. Nevertheless there is an interesting awakening. High Holy Day services are being conducted by the three largest communities (Belgrade, Zagreb and Sarajevo) with the help of Ladino speaking guest rabbis. Summer camps for young people are being organized to provide the youngsters with an appreciation of Jewish history and culture.

Even without the war, the Jewish population in Yugoslavia would have probably remained static. The almost total destruction of people over fifty and under sixteen left the Jewish community with a very small number of children. Jewish children brought up in a socialist state are susceptible to assimilation particularly when they are a small minority. Instruction in Judaism is the sole responsibility of the parents, who are often unable to meet their obligation. Who can say whether emigration to Israel, and elsewhere, and assimilation will not in fact undermine the continuity and existence of the Jewish community in Yugoslavia, one of the oldest on the European continent? Only the future can tell. Historians have stated that after May 1945 other peoples counted their war losses while the Jews counted their survivors.

Among the Jewish communities in Europe, particularly in Holland, Belgium, Luxemburg, Norway and West Germany, as well as in East Germany, Czechoslovakia, Yugoslavia and Greece, Jewish life is not what it used to be. Poland is almost without Jews ("Judenrein," only seven thousand are left). There are grounds for

[19] A term used by J. Presser in The Destruction of Dutch Jews, p. 543.

assuming and hoping that the spiritual survival of the remnant in other European countries is more promising. Some survivors had hoped after the end of the War that European Jewish communities would be rebuilt. They believed for a while in a "miracle." It proved to be an illusion. The physical rebirth of European Jewry did not occur. It was easier to overcome the Black Years of Bogdan Chmielnitski (1648-1649) revolt and massacres of Jews in Poland than the "Final Solution" of Adolf Hitler. There are still men and women among European Jews, in the West as well as in the East, who dream of the impossible. It is within human nature "to hope against hope," contra spem speramus.

The Czechoslovakian government in 1972 is proving the point; dictating to the tragically small Jewish remnant to obliterate its identity. The Czechoslovaks are making a mockery of their own history. A thousand years of Jewish culture on their soil is of no importance to the present rulers. Prague decided to follow faithfully in the footsteps of Moscow. Thus is passing the grandeur of an old world before our own eyes; sic transit gloria mundi!

PART II
History-Making Letters

History-Making Letters

Letters and Minutes Listed Chronologically

Letter from commissioners Srechko Bujas and Branko Milakovich, Sarajevo, dated November 16, 1941, No. 946/41 addressed to the Jewish Religious Community. Osijek.

Letter from commissioners Srechko Bujas and Branko Milakovich, Sarajevo, dated November 22, 1941, addressed to the Jewish Religious Community, Zagreb.

Letter from commissioners Srechko Bujas and Branko Milakovich, Sarajevo, dated November 22, 1941, addressed to the Prefect of the District, Sarajevo.

Letter from commissioners Srechko Bujas and Branko Milakovich, Sarajevo, dated November 23, 1941, No. 962/1941 addressed to the Jewish Religious Community, Zagreb.

Note attached to the minutes explaining the trip of the Prefect of
Sarajevo, Ismetbeg Gavran-Kapetanovich, to Zagreb, probably to
discuss the "final solution" of Sarajevo's Jewry.

Minutes of a meeting held in Sarajevo on November 24, 1941,
addressed to the Prefecture Vrhbosna, Sarajevo. Present were:
Commissioners Srechko Bujas, Branko Milakovich, Dr. Asim
Musakadich, Chief of the Health Department, City of Sarajevo, and
Dr. Ante Raguz, Chief of the Department of Health and Social
Welfare, District Vrhbosna, Sarajevo.

Letter from commissioners Srechko Bujas and Branko Milakovich,
Sarajevo, dated November 25, 1941, No. 971/1941 to the Jewish
Community in Zagreb.

Letter from commissioners Srechko Bujas and Branko Milakovich,
Sarajevo, dated November 26, 1941, No. 978/1941 to the Jewish
Community in Zagreb.

Letter from commissioners Srechko Bujas and Branko Milakovich,
Sarajevo, dated November 26, 1941, No. 981/41 to the Jewish
Community in Osijek.

Letter from commissioners Srechko Bujas and Branko Milakovich,
Sarajevo, dated November 27, 1941, No. 989/1941 to the Jewish
Community in Zagreb.

Letter from the Jewish Community, Zagreb, dated November 29,
1941, Dr. H-680 to the Jewish Community in Slavonski Brod.

Letter from the Jewish Community, Zagreb, dated November 29,
1941, Dr. R/R. G-676, to the Commissioners of the Jewish
Communities in Sarajevo.

Letter from the Commissioner of the Jewish Sephardic Community in Sarajevo, Srechko Bujas, Sarajevo, dated December 8,
1941 No. 1016/41 to the Jewish Community in Osijek.

Letter from the Commissioner of the Sephardic Jewish Community in Sarajevo, Srechko Bujas, Sarajevo, dated December 8,
1941, No. 1017/41, to the Jewish Communities of (a) Zagreb
(b) Osijek.

Letter from the Commissioner of the Jewish Sephardic Community in Sarajevo, Srechko Bujas, Sarajevo, dated December 9, 1941, No. 1018/41, to the Jewish Community in Osijek.

Letter from the Commissioner of the Jewish Sephardic Community, Sarajevo, Srechko Bujas, Sarajevo, dated December 10, 1941, No. 1020/41 to the Jewish Community in Osijek.

Letter from the Commissioners of the Jewish Communities in Sarajevo, Srechko Bujas, and Branko Milakovich, Sarajevo, dated December 15, 1941, No. 1029/41, to the Jewish Community in Osijek.

Letter from the Commissioners of the Jewish Communities in Sarajevo, Srechko Bujas and Branko Milakovich, Sarajevo, dated December 19, 1941, No. 1048/41 to the Jewish Community in Osijek.

Letter from the Commissioners of the Jewish Communities in Sarajevo, Srechko Bujas and Branko Milakovich, Sarajevo, dated December 21, 1941, No. 1061/41 to the Jewish Community in Osijek.

Letter from the Commissioners of the Jewish Communities in Sarajevo, Srechko Bujas and Branko Milakovich, Sarajevo, dated December 23, 1941, No. 1070/41 to the Jewish Community in Osijek.

Letter from the Commissioners of the Jewish Communities in Sarajevo, Srechko Bujas and Branko Milakovich, Sarajevo, dated December 27, 1941, No. 1101/41 to the Jewish Community in Osijek.

◆

Commissioners of the Jewish Religious Communities
in Sarajevo

Srechko Bujas, President of the District Court
Branko Milakovich, District Judge

Sarajevo, November 16, 1941

No. 946/41

To the Jewish Religious Community
Osijek

We confirm the receipt of your communication no. 746/41 of November 9th. We thank you for the detailed reports as well as for your concern for the internees and your efforts to help them.

In regard to the question of financing the groups of refugees in Chapljina and Slatina we are still of the same opinion as expressed in one of our recent letters. We are discussing it with the Jewish Community of Zagreb. As you know, the Jewish Religious Communities in Sarajevo are in a very difficult financial and material situation. Engineer Zeillinger, an emissary of the refugee group from Chapljina, saw it for himself when he was in Sarajevo on November 12th. He is now in Zagreb where he will report about our proposal and ask for direct help from the Jewish Community in Zagreb. Of course, we are not going to halt our help to the camps. We sent 150,000 KN. (kunas) for food in the camps; we are sending daily collective and individual packages with clothes and footwear for the internees in Lobor and Jasenovac. We intend, as much as conditions allow us, to continue sending money and clothing for the internees. The collecting of goods and money for the internment camps is being carried on very actively and is having relatively good results. Among other things, we have started an action whose purpose is to collect some sewing machines. We will write to you later about the outcome of our effort.

In regard to all this, we are thinking of sending our representatives to the provinces as well as to Osijek and Zagreb. The problem is that the representatives of the Jewish Communities in Sarajevo cannot, at the present time, obtain permission for their officials to travel. As soon as we solve this problem of the travel permits, we will send our representatives to the country, Osijek and Zagreb.

We were pleased to learn from your report that the food distribution in the camp at Jasenovac has been solved in a satisfactory way.

We received 1,000 postcards to be used when writing to the internees at Jasenovac. However, that number of postcards is not sufficient to satisfy the needs. There are now more than 1,300 internees from Sarajevo in Jasenovac. Having only 1,000 postcards at our disposal, we cannot give a postcard to each family that has a member in Jasenovac. Please, speak to the command of the camp to change the present system of correspondence, so that the internees would be allowed to write first and then receive replies from their families. This way many misunderstandings in correspondence could be eliminated.

We would like to inform you that the committee in charge of helping the internees of the Greek Orthodox faith—and we cooperate, with the permission of the authorities, with that committee—asked us to get for them a list of names and previous addresses of the internees of the Greek Orthodox faith and postcards for their families. We believe that in order to improve our cooperation with the Greek Orthodox, their very justified demand should be given urgent attention. Incidentally, there are numerous people of the Greek Orthodox faith in Sarajevo and we expect them also to help us.

We repeat, this cooperation with the Greek Orthodox is taking place with the permission of the police authorities and the commander of the camp, Mr. Luburich. All is done with the knowledge and approval of the Ustashi Police Department and its Jewish section.

Please send us a list with the names of the interned Jews from Sarajevo. There are approximately 1,300 Jews in Jasenovac now. Thus far, we have not received any information about them. The list of the internees in Jasenovac which we have received, has only sixteen names of Jews from Sarajevo.

Expecting your reply to all questions discussed, we remain respectfully yours,

> Srechko Bujas,
> President of the District Court
> Branko Milakovich,
> District Judge

Commissioners of the Jewish Religious Communities in Sarajevo

Srechko Bujas, President of the District Court
Branko Milakovich, District Judge

Sarajevo, November 22, 1941

To the Jewish Religious Community
Zagreb

In connection with our previous letters which we wrote to you, we would like to add and to inform you that the situation of the internees in Sarajevo is becoming very difficult and complicated.

First of all, our Communities are not officially recognized anymore. Their existence is merely tolerated. There is no contact with the authorities whatsoever. It is true that on our own initiative and out of our sense of responsibility to the members of our community, we are providing them with food and help. Without our help, they would suffer from starvation and from a cold, severe winter. It is a picture of misery and suffering. There are hundreds of sick, crippled, paralyzed and blind; babies, old people over seventy. In short people who, under normal circumstances would have been taken care of. They live under frightening unhygienic conditions, lying on the bare floors. We are unable even to take out those who are very sick and send them to their homes or to the hospital.

The apartments of all the internees are sealed. The authorities sealed their apartments regardless of whether all members of the families were at home at the time when the round-up took place. Due to these circumstances many are left without any possessions whatsoever.

Facing such a terrible situation, without a sufficient number of clerks and officials; having no freedom of movement whatsoever, and fearing for the freedom of that small number of our officials, none of which has either his home or his family anymore, we are addressing and asking you to intervene urgently with the authorities in Zagreb in order to normalize and ease this situation. If it is not possible to return all the internees to their homes, then, at least a selection should be made so that those be freed who, under no conditions should have been interned. In fact, the majority of the interned in the city fall into that category. Furthermore, there is an immediate danger of infectious disease which will spread with terrible speed because too many people are packed into very small living quarters.

Finally, our financial situation is such that we cannot shelter and feed the internees for more than ten days. We consider it necessary that you discuss, with the authorities in Zagreb, the problem of financing and the provision of food for all the internees. We think that the problem of financing should not, under any circumstances, become a burden of the Jewish communities alone.

We ask you to consider this, (let us call it, Sarajevo's problem) as a very urgent matter and devote all your efforts and immediate attention to it.

Respectfully yours,

Branko Milakovich,
District Judge

Commissioners of the Jewish Religious Communities in Sarajevo

Srechko Bujas, President of the District Court
Branko Milakovich, District Judge

Sarajevo, November 22, 1941

To the Prefect (of the District of Sarajevo)
Sarajevo

Being unable to get in touch with the Police authorities of the District (of Sarajevo), we have no choice but to address you with a request that you take urgent steps which would help to normalize the situation which is, as things stand now, leading toward a tragedy. The conditions under which our communities exist are unbearable. We have decided to write to you as commissioners of the Jewish Communities, as patriots and loyal Croats, as Christians and human beings, who have piety and compassion for the weak and sick and those who badly need help.

Before we suggest to you concrete measures which are absolutely necessary, let us first familiarize you with the history of the events.

On Sunday, November 16th, the general round-up of the Jews started. After having been transported many times from place to place, the summoned are still in Sarajevo. The round-up continued on Monday and Tuesday. In that way about 2,000 people were summoned to the concentration center which at that time was located in the German Camp. About 1,000 were transported from the city of Sarajevo. The rest had to be transported back to the city on Friday, November 21st. There are now only a few hundred Jews in the city who have not been interned.

The Police authorities of the District (of Sarajevo) were not able to shelter the internees and asked us to do that. We are aware that we should be doing all we can in sheltering these people, and this in spite of the *negative* attitude shown by the Police towards the Jewish Communities. We vacated and cleaned the only two remaining synagogues in order to shelter the internees. We also helped in transporting the internees back to the city.

Out of the 1,000 internees, 900 are women and children. A great number of them are sick and should be hospitalized. Among the internees are many pregnant women, paralyzed and blind people, newly-born babies up to 15 days old. We can not describe the unhappiness and misery which has fallen upon these people.

Today is the seventh day since the internment started; and not a single meal has been given to these helpless people, not even a piece of bread, nothing to keep them alive.

Hygienic conditions are very inadequate, there is a very real danger of the spread of infectious disease, which, if it takes place, will surely spread into neighboring areas and the city of Sarajevo herself.

We have already mentioned above that the Jewish Communities are not recognized anymore. Their functioning is merely tolerated. In spite of that and regardless of the fact that our officials are not protected in any way, we have provided food and shelter for all the internees from the first day of their internment. Of course, we did all we could under the circumstances and with our very limited capacity.

All the internees are in the city now. But we do not have contact with the authorities, we are unable to function freely, our financial resources are very limited. That is why we seek your help and call upon you to do all that can be done in order to improve the situation.

The following measures should be taken, urgently, and we would appreciate it if you could submit these proposals, together with this letter, to the authorized Ministry for a decision.

1) To enable the further functioning of Sarajevo's Jewish Communities in accordance with the practice in the Independent State of Croatia. The communities should be entitled, in the framework of the law, to establish and maintain regular contact with the authorities as well as with the internees for whom both the authorities and the Jewish Communities should care, particularly as far as provision of food and medical attention are concerned.

2) Officials of the Jewish Communities should be protected and secure in carrying out their duties. They should be allowed to live in their apartments and be freed from internment.

3) Jewish Communities should be allowed, within the limits of the law, to collect revenues and contributions from the

Jewish shops and households. The Communities are in a very difficult financial situation.

4) To take necessary steps to halt further internment of Jews from Sarajevo till the present situation is resolved. If there is going to be more internment anyway, then it should be done in a more humane way, at least. As we already mentioned earlier, the present internees are almost exclusively old men and women, newborn babies, children, sick people and invalids.

In expectation of a solution which will make us all feel better about this problem and which will prevent the otherwise inevitable destruction of these people, we thank you in advance and remain

READY FOR THE HOMELAND!

――――◆◇◆――――

**Commissioners of the Jewish Religious Communities
in Sarajevo**

**Srechko Bujas, President of the District Court
Branko Milakovich, District Judge**

Sarajevo, November 23, 1941

No. 962/1941
To the Jewish Religious Community
Zagreb

It has been eight days since a terrible tragedy has befallen Sarajevo's Jewish Community. There are no words to describe it. Being in total uncertainty, without direct contact with the Chief of the Police Department, left in the hands of unfortunate fate, we are writing to you. We are hoping very much that you will do all you can for these wretched and unhappy people, many of whom will these days become victims of the scythe of death, caused by sickness and disease, and might be entirely destroyed.

For eight days already these people are left without any care, without medication, without hot meals, without milk for children; in one word—without anything. They live in terrible filth which threatens to develop into a disease, spreading over the city.

Yesterday we saw the Prefect and presented to him our memorandum, a copy of which is attached to this letter. During our long conversation with the Prefect, we informed him about the extremely difficult situation and asked him to intervene urgently with the authorities in Zagreb. The Prefect showed considerable understanding for our work and needs and promised to submit our proposals immediately by radiogram to the Ministry in Zagreb. He will also send our memorandum by mail (to Zagreb). We urge you to do as much as you can, using this information.

We have learned that there exists a new camp for women near Novi Marof, where women from the last Sarajevo contingent and some from Lobor have been sent. We would like to know more about the camp in Novi Marof. What is the exact location of the camp? What are the food provisions? What is the capacity of the camp? We have been informed from a few sources that the last contingent of women will be returned to Sarajevo. However, it has not arrived here.

We need these days daily and immediate information about your actions and efforts concerning not only our (Sarajevo's) problem, but other problems as well, which are of importance for the Jewish Communities. Especially, write us about the problem of the food and packages for Jasenovac.

Respectfully yours,
Srechko Bujas, President of the District Court

Express-Registered

Attached is a copy of minutes taken upon a verbal request made by the Prefect of the District of Vrhbosna, after an inspection of the internees and their lodgings was made by an ad hoc commission.

P.S. We are informing you that today Mr. Ismetbeg Gavran-Kapetanovich, the Prefect of the District of Sarajevo, set out for Zagreb. His trip is probably connected with the question of the Sarajevo Jews. Try to get in touch with him while the Prefect is in Zagreb and with the authorities as well. Among other things insist especially on the permission to merge the Jewish communities and charitable organizations.

MINUTES

Taken upon a verbal request by the Prefect of the District of Vrhbosna (at the meeting held) in Sarajevo on November 24, 1941.

Present: Srechko Bujas, President of the District Court of Sarajevo, Commissioner of the Sephardic Jewish Community in Sarajevo, by a decree of the Poglavnik's Commission in Sarajevo, No. 227/41 of May 14, 1941; Branko Milakovich, judge of the District Court of Sarajevo, Commissioner of the Ashkenazic Jewish Community in Sarajevo, by a decree of the Poglavnik's Commission in Sarajevo No. 1420/41 of May 31, 1941; Dr. Asim Musakadich, Chief of the Health Department at the city of Sarajevo; and, Dr. Ante Raguz, Chief of the Department of Health and Social Welfare of the District Vrhbosna in Sarajevo.

Subject: Inspection of the living quarters of the interned Jews from Sarajevo and inspection of the contingent of internees which was returned to Sarajevo from Zagreb.

It was established that a part of the interned Jews, about 400 women and children, are housed in the old Jewish Synagogue, at Dr. Ante Pavelich St.; another group, about 300 women and children and some men, in the building "La Benevolencija." Also, an inspection was made of the contingent of women and children returned to Sarajevo, which arrived from Zagreb this morning, and is now at the main railroad station.

During the inspection the following was found: The synagogues, which are absolutely unsuitable for lodgings, are in a terrible mess, filth everywhere, poor ventilation. There are no restrooms in the temples; people use the yard instead. There are no beds, or any accommodations of that kind. The internees, crowded together, lie or sit on the floors and are very miserable. There are many chronically sick among them: some had various operations just before having been interned, some suffer from acute illnesses like whooping cough and enteritis. Certain infectious diseases have started developing, like scabies and a contagious throat disease. Lice too, have been noted. During the inspection very old men and women were seen. They were totally helpless, unable to move, some paralyzed, blind and insane. There is also a considerable number of newborn babies and pregnant women. Hygienic conditions are intolerable. The preconditions exist for a rapid spread of disease.

The authorities have not provided the internees with any kind of regular feeding. Provisions of the food depends entirely on the Jewish Religious Communities and some occasional donors. The Jewish Community does not have any source of income. And even so, its efforts to provide the internees with basic food needs are obstructed by the Police authorities, by not granting freedom of movement to officials and clerks of the Community.

The internees sent back from Zagreb were found at the main railroad station in railroad cars. They have been there for eight days without food or water. Six hundred internees are in 12 freight cars. Their health is in a desperate state. Many cases of acute and infectious diseases were found. Many women suffer from swollen legs.

On the basis of our findings—and in order to prevent the spread of the infectious diseases over the whole city—we believe that it is absolutely necessary to send those who are very sick to hospitals, as well as those who suffer from infectious diseases. The rest of the internees should be sent to their homes in Sarajevo until the authorities will build appropriate camps for them.

We believe this is the only possible solution to the present situation.

READY FOR THE HOMELAND!

Sarajevo, November 24, 1941
Minutes recorded by Mustafa (last name illegible)

        Members:
1. Srechko Bujas
2. Branko Milakovich
3. Dr. Ante Raguz
4. Dr. Asim Musakadich

Commissioners of the Jewish Religious Communities
in Sarajevo

Srechko Bujas, President of the District Court
Branko Milakovich, District Judge

Sarajevo, November 25, 1941

No. 971/1941
To the Jewish Religious Community
Zagreb

We confirm the receipt of your letter of November 21, Dr. G/676/1941.

We would like to inform you briefly about the situation in our communities as it stands today.

The contingent of about 700 women and children arrived yesterday in Sarajevo. These people are placed in a building of an elementary school and in the apartment house, "La Benevolencija." There are now about 1,600 interned Jews in Sarajevo. Only 90 of them are men. About 500 Jews in the city still have freedom of movement, out of which only 70-80 are males.

The Jewish religious communities take care of the internees, and provide them with food. The lodgings, where the internees are placed, are sanitarily unsuitable. The rooms are small; they are not intended for lodgings. Among the internees are many sick and helpless people, small children and many old women.

We do not know what is going to happen to the internees. We are waiting for a decision to be made by the authorities.

In brief, the situation of the internees is extremely difficult. We can not see any remedy, unless a quick and resolute solution is found soon. We think that at the present moment the situation could be improved only if the internees were allowed to go back to their homes. This is a solution which should be insisted upon, and we ask you to work in that direction with the authorities in Zagreb.

The question of the further existence of the Jewish Community in Sarajevo is also at stake. All Jews in Sarajevo have become so poor that we can not see any way of solving the economic problems of the Jews in our communities.

If the proposals which we submitted to the Prefect in Sarajevo in our memorandum of November 22, 1941 (we have sent a copy to you) had materialized, we think that the situation could have been improved. We would like to add to those proposals the following. In order to enable the future existence of the Jewish Communities, they should merge with other (Jewish) charitable institutions. In that way the Communities would be in charge of the property of the charitable institutions. That property is not of too much value altogether. It consists of just a few houses and a small amount of money. But, even with these resources, it would be possible to provide some help to the Jews in Sarajevo. Their requests for help are minimal and the majority of them belong to the most impoverished of the city's population.

We ask you to take all necessary steps with the authorities (in Zagreb) that might help to accept our proposals.

We agree that it is very necessary and urgent to have a meeting of the representatives of the Jewish communities of Zagreb, Osijek and Sarajevo. At that meeting the problems of the internees should be discussed. However, the delegates from Sarajevo cannot obtain permission yet to travel. We asked the Police Department here whether they have received a telegram from Zagreb regarding the issuing of permission to travel (for our representatives). The answer was, "No, they did not receive such an order." Please urge the authorities in the Jewish section to issue the necessary permission for travel for our representatives.

We would like to emphasize again that all this is very urgent and that only a resolute intervention with the authorities could save the miserable remnants of what used to be the Jewish community in Sarajevo.

Expecting your urgent intervention with the authorities in Zagreb and thanking you for all you did for the Jewish internees during their stay in Zagreb, we remain

Respectfully yours,

Branko Milakovich,
District Judge

Commissioners of the Jewish Religious Communities in Sarajevo

Srechko Bujas, President of the District Court
Branko Milakovich, District Judge

Sarajevo, November 26, 1941

No. 978/1941
To the Jewish Religious Community
Zagreb

We would like to ask you again to write to us daily and inform us in detail about the steps you are undertaking in behalf of our cause.

Yesterday, the Chief of the Police Department returned (from Zagreb) to Sarajevo. We expected that immediately after his return, the internees would be sent to their homes. Presently, they are placed in four buildings, none of which is suitable for lodgings. Although 11 days have passed since these people have been interned, even the problem of the sleeping accommodations has not been solved. There is already a case of contagious throat disease, a number of cases of scabies, also a case of insanity. An epidemic of all kinds of contagious diseases could be expected at any moment. But, hardly anything has been done about it. The only thing which is supposed to have taken place today is the release of very old women. Actually, the reason for their release is that the public school where they are stationed must now be vacated. Apparently, the old women are not going to be sent to their homes, but to various other places.

The feeding of over 1,500 internees, provision of food, medical supplies and over-all care for the internees is connected with enormous difficulties. The capacity of our kitchen is at most 500 meals. In spite of that, we are somehow managing to feed all internees. However, we will not be able to carry on even for a short period of time. We would like to emphasize that the Police authorities have not distributed a single meal, nor did they provide the internees with any other basic necessities.

We informed you through our daily communications of the conditions here, and today, while hoping for a positive solution which might come from Zagreb, we are sending to you this last call for help. If the help does not come promptly a catastrophe is inevitable. To illustrate: the contingent of 600 women which was returned to Sarajevo, spent seven long days at the railroad in cars, without being permitted to leave the wagons, without washing, and for the most part without any food. There is no need to explain in what shape and condition these people are.

It is becoming more and more difficult for our Community to function and perform its duties. All but one of the Community's officials and clerks are separated from their families, and deprived of their apartments. They lack clothing and footwear. They sleep on the floors of our office. They work tirelessly from early in the morning till late in the night. We can not do anything for them. We are unable to place them in apartments, nor have we succeeded in having their families returned to them. We can not do anything about their basic safety. Under such conditions, the existence of our Community also approaches its end.

We have learned from some sources that one of these days women from the camp in Lobor will be returned to Sarajevo. Please, could you keep them for a while in Zagreb till the situation here has improved? We do not know what to do anymore with the internees already here. Everything is so miserable and difficult.

We believe it is very important that our representatives should go to Zagreb. As far as our commissioner Mr. Milakovich is concerned, it is necessary to get permission for him to be absent from Sarajevo for five days. This permission should be obtained from the Jewish Section of the Ministry of Justice. That is needed because judges cannot leave their working assignments without the permission of the Ministry of Justice. As far as our officials and clerks are concerned, a radiogram or an official request should be sent to the Police Department of the District of Sarajevo in order to obtain for them permission to travel.

Respectfully,

Srechko Bujas,
President of the District Court

Commissioners of the Jewish Religious Communities
in Sarajevo

Srechko Bujas, President of the District Court
Branko Milakovich, District Judge

No. 981/41   Sarajevo, November 26, 1941
  To the Jewish Religious Community
                   Osijek
We confirm your communication of November 23, No. 870/41.

We can see from your letter that you are well informed about the internment of the Sarajevo Jews. We would like to thank you for sending your representative, Mr. Selvyn Levi, to Slavonski Brod in order to help the internees from Sarajevo.

We would like to inform you that the contingent of women, which you mentioned in your letter, arrived in Sarajevo on Monday, November 24th. These women are now, together with the other Jewish internees from Sarajevo, placed in four buildings. We do not know what is going to happen to them. We are waiting for the decision of the authorities. The future of the internees depends on that decision.

There are today about 1,500 Jews in internment in Sarajevo. About 500-600 Jews are still free in the city. Among them are only about 160-170 males.

All that the Jewish Communities in Sarajevo are doing now is centered around the provision of food for the internees and their general care. We are devoting most of our time to that problem. This is very difficult to solve because we do not have enough manpower for all that, and lack financial means to get food. As soon as we solve this problem, we will put our efforts into actions which would strengthen the Jewish Community of Sarajevo. We would then start with activities dealing with the care of the internees in the camps.

Once again we thank you for your care for the Sarajevo internees.

We remain respectfully yours,

Srechko Bujas, President of the District Court
Branko Milakovich, District Judge

Commissioners of the Jewish Religious Communities in Sarajevo

Srechko Bujas, President of the District Court
Branko Milakovich, District Judge

No. 989/1941   Sarajevo, November 27, 1941

To the Jewish Religious Community
Zagreb

This is to inform you of the situation of the internees as we see it, on the basis of information and reports gathered today. Basically, the internees are in the same situation as they were before. The conditions under which they live have not improved at all. Yesterday and today some very old people were released, but they were not allowed to return to their homes. They have been released under the condition that they find shelter for and by themselves, and do not go back to their homes. In other words, they did not get back the keys of their apartments, nor permission to enter their apartments, which are still officially sealed. What is new is that some new internees, who were arrested these days for various reasons, have been placed in the buildings with the previous prisoners.

We do not know what the fate of the internees is going to be. We are waiting for the decisions to be made by the authorities. We do not know exactly who is supposed to make the decisions and what the result will be. We are extremely worried about the internees, first of all because we do not know what is going to happen to them. Also, we do not know how long we can provide them with food and medical care. Medical care is our special concern because there are cases of serious illness. A great number of people suffer from colds, catarrh, throat infections and other illnesses.

Again we ask you to take all necessary steps to find a quick solution to this problem. We expect you to write us all you know regarding the internees and their fate. Please write us in detail and more often.

Expecting your prompt reply, we remain, respectfully yours,

Branko Milakovich, District Judge
Srechko Bujas, President of the District Court

November 29, 1941

"dr."/H-680
To the Jewish Religious Community
Brod

We confirm the receipt of your communication No. 113 of November 25th regarding the financial situation of your community; and the information concerning problems of contributions to the Jewish Communities through the commissioners of the Jewish mercantile firms. Unfortunately, we have to inform you that all our efforts to find a uniform solution for the whole country, which would enable the Jewish Communities to have a considerable source of income and provide them with the necessary funds for the fulfillment of their responsible and difficult tasks, have brought no positive results. The whole problem is still under discussion, and we are doing all we can in order to find a satisfactory solution.

Attached to this letter are copies of letters which we have sent today to the distinguished Jewish Communities in Sarajevo and Osijek, so you can learn what has been done with regard to the solution of the problem of the Sarajevo internees. As soon as more accurate information about the contingent from Sarajevo and its passage through Brod becomes available, we will inform you of it. You will have to organize, receive and prepare food for the contingent of the internees. If it proves to be necessary and possible, representatives of Sarajevo's and Osijek's Communities will be sent to Brod in order to help you organize, receive and provide food for the contingent from Sarajevo.

We will also try to supply you with some money for that purpose.

Chairman: Secretary:
Signature illegible   Signature illegible
                    Seal
            Jewish Religious Community
                   Zagreb

Copies attached:
Express-Registered

November 29, 1941

Dr. R/RG-676

To the Messrs: Commissioners of the Jewish Religious Communities   *Sarajevo*

We received yesterday your letter no. 978 of November 26th. Today we received the letter of November 27th. This is to reply briefly to these letters and to inform you what we have found out from the Jewish Section regarding the further fate of the interned women and children from Sarajevo.

A decision was made last night that all interned Jewish women and children will, without any delay, be sent to Osijek and interned there. Those who are gravely sick and totally exhausted, due to their old age or other causes, are not going to be sent to Osijek. Whether the internees are going to be lodged at one place or, partly at Jewish homes, will depend on the authorities in Osijek and the possibilities of sheltering the internees in Osijek. That is basically all we could find out. Probably there are not any more detailed plans and orders at the present time.

Please get in touch with the authorities in Sarajevo regarding this matter. Try to find out how the whole operation is going to be executed and other related information. As soon as you find this out, write us so that we can inform the Jewish Community in Osijek which will have to take care of shelter and food for the internees. Of course, it will be necessary to meet this contingent and provide it with food during its passage and stay in Brod.

It is hardly necessary to tell you that during these ten days or so, which are extremely difficult for Sarajevo's Jews, we have been tirelessly presenting the problems to the Jewish Section. We have submitted copies of your reports and begged for intervention and help. We wrote you about all that and about the unsatisfactory results in all our efforts. Now that finally the decision has been made, we hope that the situation will improve, although neither you nor we expected any improvement in that matter.

In accordance with your earlier proposal and upon our request, the Jewish Section of the Ministry of Justice sent a telegram to the District Police Department in Sarajevo, instructing them to issue a permission for travel both for the commissioners of the Jewish

Communities in Sarajevo and for the clerks, Dr. M. Papo and Josef Levi. We urgently asked the Jewish Section to get the permission from the Ministry of Justice. They promised us they would do that, and told us that the Ministry will send the telegram to Sarajevo.

The permissions for travel will be granted for traveling to Zagreb and Osijek because there might be a need to go to Osijek to see how and where to place the internees, and discuss matters regarding the provision of food, collecting funds, etc. Before the trip to Osijek, a conference should be held in Zagreb with the delegates from the community of Osijek. We would ask them to come to Zagreb as soon as we receive information about the arrival here of your delegates.

We are sending a copy of this letter to the Jewish Community in Osijek.

We expect urgent information from you regarding the transportation and movement of the contingent of internees. Please write directly to the Jewish Religious Community in Brod na Savi and give them the necessary information. Write to: Dr. Milan Pollak, Brod, Starchevicheva 44. We will send also a copy of this letter to them.

Chairman: Secretary
                                   Signature illegible
                        Seal
              Jewish Religious Community
                      Zagreb

Express-Registered!

P.S. Attached are copies of our letters to the Jewish Communities in Osijek and Brod.

Commissioner of the Jewish Sephardic Community in Sarajevo
Srechko Bujas, President of the District Court

No. 1016/41   Sarajevo, December 8, 1941

To the Jewish Religious Community
Osijek

On the basis of today's reports about the interned Jews of Sarajevo, I would like to inform you about the latest developments.

First of all I would like to thank you for your labor and the readiness with which you took care of the last transport of Sarajevo's internees. I learned from Slavonski Brod that you sent your representatives all the way to Brod and that they helped, on that occasion, the interned women and children. I have also been informed that you helped a great deal in accommodating the interned women in Djakovo. Information which we received concerning Djakovo is quite sketchy and we would appreciate it if you could let us know when the internees arrived in Djakovo, where they are placed and under whose supervision. Tell us more about their lodgings, about your contact with the internees and other matters regarding the camp in Djakovo.

As you know, our representatives were invited to go to Zagreb and we are informed that they will be in Osijek either on Tuesday or Wednesday.

Since the last transport, about 140 internees have remained in the building "La Benevolencija." Half of them are men and half of them are women, who could not be transported due to their physical exhaustion. Yesterday, on Sunday, the round-up of Jews continued. About 100 persons, both males and females were gathered. Today, and it is now 10:30 P.M., no round-up has taken place. We do not know whether further round-ups and internments of the Jews will continue. All internees, previous and new, that is the 140 left from the last transport and the 100 new arrivals are placed in the building "La Benevolencija."

We thank you again for your effort in helping the internees and in expectation of news from you, I remain,

Respectfully yours,
Commissioner of the Jewish Sephardic
Community in Sarajevo
Srechko Bujas, President of the District Court

Commissioner of the Sephardic Jewish Community in Sarajevo

Srechko Bujas, President of the District Court

Sarajevo, December 8, 1941

No. 1017/41

To the Jewish Religious Communities
    a. Zagreb
    b. Osijek

According to the latest information concerning the internment of the Jews in Sarajevo, and knowing about your help regarding the internees, this is to inform you that today no change has taken place. I emphasize that we had, today, no round-up of Jews. Therefore, the number of internees in the building "La Benevolencija" remains the same. To add, we do not know at all what the fate of the Jewish Community in Sarajevo will be.

Expecting news from you, I remain

Respectfully yours,

Commissioner of the Jewish Sephardic
Community in Sarajevo

Srechko Bujas,
President of the District Court

Commissioner of the Jewish Sephardic Community
in Sarajevo

Srechko Bujas, President of the District Court

Sarajevo, December 9, 1941

No. 1018/41

To the Jewish Religious Community
Osijek

We confirm the receipt of your letter of December 6th, a letter from the committee for provisions for the camps no. 1043/41, and a communication No. 1 from the administration of the Concentration Camp in Djakovo.

I lack words to commend your work on behalf of the women internees from Sarajevo. On the basis of the letters mentioned above, I can conclude that the Jewish Community in Osijek acted in a highly organized way and with great devotion to secure living quarters for the women internees. All I can do now is to express my gratitude for all your efforts. I promise you that I will, in cooperation with the commissioner for the Jewish Ashkenazic Community in Sarajevo, do all I can, in order to ease your work regarding the care of the confined women in Djakovo.

I believe that the delegates from Sarajevo will arrive in Osijek in a few days. They might arrive before you receive this letter, and you will have an opportunity to work out programs for future activity regarding the new camp for women. In case our delegates are prevented from going to Osijek, I will write to you this week in full detail about the questions you raised regarding the camp in Djakovo.

I believe that proper functioning of the camp depends on good organization and the Jewish Communities in Sarajevo will try to get permission to send a man who would help you in this action.

Again I thank you for the unselfish and good work shown through your care of the women internees from Sarajevo, and I remain

Respectfully,

Commissioner of the Jewish Sephardic
Community in Sarajevo
Srechko Bujas

Commissioner of the Jewish Sephardic Community in Sarajevo

Srechko Bujas, President of the District Court

Sarajevo, December 10, 1941

No. 1020/41

To the Jewish Religious Community
Osijek

I believe that our delegates are already in your city and that you are discussing with them all questions regarding the new camp for women in Djakovo.

There are no changes here since my last letter. There have not been any new round-ups yesterday and today. The number of the internees in the building "La Benevolencija" remained the same. Presently there is no word about transporting this group of internees. I do not know what will happen to them.

Our community provides the internees with food and takes care of their needs such as firewood, medications, etc.

When you receive this letter and our delegates are in Osijek, please inform them of its content. Tell them also that the District Police Department, when gathering the Jews, is considering whether somebody is an official of the Jewish Community or an official's family member. The Police asked me to inform them whether there are any officials of the Jewish Community or members of their families in the building "La Benevolencija." None of our officials has been interned. However, a daughter of an official was interned. We have intervened on her behalf, but she is still in "La Benevolencija."

Expecting news from you and thanking you for your work, I remain

Respectfully yours,

Commissioner of the Jewish Sephardic
Community in Sarajevo
Srechko Bujas,
President of the District Court

Commissioners of the Jewish Communities
in Sarajevo
Srechko Bujas, President of the District Court
Branko Milakovich, District Judge

No. 1029/41   Sarajevo, December 15, 1941

To the Jewish Religious Community
Osijek

After our representatives returned from their trip, where they had an opportunity to meet your representatives, we have the pleasant duty to express once again our deep appreciation and gratitude for your truly devoted and unselfish work manifested in the action of your people from the president to the last co-worker.

It was a real and true pleasure to see how much you accomplished within the span of a few days, at your disposal, in setting up the camp in Djakovo. It was not less impressive and pleasant to listen to your plans for further action which will, we are convinced, bring positive results. The energy and determination which is characteristic of your work are a guarantee for success.

It would be unnecessary to mention individual names, but in the name of all of us, we thank you very, very much and we express our deep appreciation to you.

We will do on our part all we possibly can to help you in your noble efforts. We have already taken steps, in agreement with our conversation, to send two of our clerks to Djakovo. We will inform you about the result of this attempt.

Please write to us more frequently and in detail, if possible, about all matters concerning the conditions in the camp in Djakovo.

The situation in Sarajevo has remained unchanged. Every day a few families are taken and interned in the building "La Benevolencija" which serves as a local camp. We do not know what the future of the internees will be; where they are going to be sent, etc.

We have another request. Please send us precise lists of the children and the homes where they are being placed. Indicate, on the lists, the parents' names and surnames, and their addresses in Sarajevo.

Respectfully yours,

Srechko Bujas, President of the District Court
Branko Milakovich, District Judge

Commissioners of the Jewish Communities
in Sarajevo

Srechko Bujas, President of the District Court
Branko Milakovich, District Judge

Sarajevo, December 19, 1941

No. 1048/41
    To the Jewish Religious Community
                    Osijek
We confirm the receipt of your letter of December 15th. First of all we ask you to inform us immediately and in detail about the camp in Djakovo. It is of great interest to us. We would like to know about the administration of the camp and about the chance that it will be administered by your community. Also, let us know about the questions of correspondence with the women internees and arrangements in regard to sending packages. What are the possibilities for placing more internees in the camp? We have learned that new contingents of men, women, and children will soon be transported from Sarajevo. Apparently the women and children will be sent to Djakovo. When our representatives were in Osijek and Djakovo they found out that the camp was already overcrowded and that there was no possibility of adding even a small number of internees. We also agreed then that you as well as the Police authorities of the District of Osijek will urgently inform the authorities in Zagreb about that. The contingents from Sarajevo would number 400-500 women and children, at least. If you have not done anything regarding this matter, please do take urgent steps as soon as possible.

As we wrote to you before, we are trying to send two of our Community officials to Djakovo. Because of very special conditions in Sarajevo, we have to act extremely cautiously. Before sending our officials to Djakovo, we would like to receive an answer from you about the questions raised above, especially the question of the administration of the camp.

We sent today a letter to the Community in Zagreb regarding the money order of 10,000 Kn. (kunas) appropriated to you by the Community of Tuzla. In our reply to the Community of Zagreb we wrote, "Regarding the sum (of money) which the Community of Tuzla sent to the Community of Osijek we want to point out that to the best of our knowledge, this is not the only monetary contribution sent from our region to Osijek. The best way to regulate this would be: the Community in Osijek would give us credit for all amounts received, so far, and formally acknowledge the sums received in the future provided that the total amount of received money from our territory is, again formally, taken into consideration when distributing the expenses of financing the camp." We hope this solution is agreeable also to you.

We will be waiting for a prompt response from you.

Respectfully yours,

Commissioners for the Jewish
Communities in Sarajevo
Srechko Bujas
Branko Milakovich

Commissioners of the Jewish Communities
in Sarajevo

Srechko Bujas, President of the District Court
Branko Milakovich, District Judge

Sarajevo, December 21, 1941

No. 1061/41
To the Jewish Religious Community
Osijek

This is to inform you that this evening two transports of internees will depart from Sarajevo. One, consisting of women and children, is apparently going to be sent to Djakovo. The other, consisting of men will, as far as we know, be sent to Jasenovac. We believe there are about 500 women, although we are not sure that the number is definite. There will be about 100 men.

Yesterday, we informed urgently the community in Brod about these transports and asked them to phone you about the same matter.

We are convinced that you will undertake all necessary steps in order to shelter the new internees.

The tendency is to deport more people from Sarajevo. The internees would be mostly women and children. Due to the fact that there are no other camps which could take in large numbers of female internees, the only place for them would be Djakovo. It is necessary that you inform the authorities of the conditions in the camp in Djakovo. Emphasize the impossibility of further crowding the camp. If you convince them, further deterioration of conditions in the camp could be prevented. Possibly further deportation of women and children from Sarajevo could be halted, at least for the present time, during this winter. It was clearly established during the stay of our representatives in Djakovo that there is not enough room in the camp for those already there. The internees who will leave tonight from Sarajevo will be sent there, and after that more and more internees might be sent to the same camp as well.

In connection with our communication, no. 1048/41, of December 19th, we ask you again to inform us urgently about the situation in the camp and answer all other questions raised in that letter.

We are still trying to get permission to send two of our Jewish officials to Djakovo. Their assignment would be to take care, together with you, of the camp's needs. We wrote about this to Zagreb. We believe that the Community in Zagreb will be successful in arranging everything that is needed for our representatives to travel to Osijek and Djakovo.

We thank you again for all you have done in helping the internees from Sarajevo.

We remain respectfully yours,

Commissioner for the Jewish
Community in Sarajevo

Commissioners of the Jewish Communities in Sarajevo

Srechko Bujas, President of the District Court Branko Milakovich, District Judge

Sarajevo, December 23, 1941

No. 1070/41

To the Jewish Religious Community
Osijek

Last night a new contingent of Jews was deported from Sarajevo. In the transport are about 800 women and children, who are being sent to Djakovo. About 200 men are being sent to Jasenovac.

We are extremely worried about the fate of the women internees because we assume that they cannot be placed in the Djakovo camp. We are afraid of the repetition of the situation with an earlier transport of women, who after seven days of traveling were sent back to Sarajevo. We emphasize that the number of very old and very sick women in this contingent is more than 200. The transport should be disinfected, if there is a possibility to do it.

Following the order of the Sarajevo Police Department in both of our Communities, only six officials and clerks have remained at their posts.

Today we have proposed to the Community in Zagreb that due to the new situation, a conference with the representatives of the three communities should take place. Please, discuss the question of the place of the conference, and other details connected with it, with the Community in Zagreb.

Please, inform us most urgently about the fate of the contingent. What has been done and what will be done with it?

We thank you in advance for all you will do in order to ease the fate of the internees.

Respectfully,

Branko Milakovich

Commissioners of the Jewish Communities in Sarajevo

Srechko Bujas, President of the District Court
Branko Milakovich, District Judge

Sarajevo, December 27, 1941

No. 1101/41

To the Jewish Religious Community
Osijek I

We have not received lately any news from you. That surprises and worries us very much. In our letter of December 19th, we asked you to inform us in detail regarding everything concerning the camp in Djakovo. We asked especially that you write us about the administration of the camp and your participation in it. Also, the questions about the organization of the camp, correspondence with the internees, possibilities of sending packages and other questions have remained unanswered.

We still have no information about the contingent of women and children which was sent from Sarajevo on the night between December 23rd and 24th. Apparently this transport was sent to Djakovo. Please let us know where and how the women from this transport have been placed.

We would appreciate it very much if you would send us, as soon as possible, a list of women internees in Djakovo.

All necessary steps have been taken to send to Djakovo our Jewish clerks, appointed to work with you. We hope that in 2-3 days they might be on their way to Djakovo, where they would assume their new duties.

Expecting urgent news from you, we remain,

Respectfully yours,

Srechko Bujas
Branko Milakovich

Such was the tragic journey of a people, most of whom were only interested in their communities, their families, their homes. The symbolic mausoleum of the annihilated Sephardim is a great pyramid of white stone on top of the Sephardic cemetery in Sarajevo. The inscription reads: "To the Jews who fell as fighters against and victims of fascism—Jasenovac—Stara Gradishka—Djakovo—Jadovno—Loborgrad—Auschwitz—Bergen-Belsen."

May the memory of the martyrs live on forever. Their names, among others, were: Abinun, Albahari, Altarac, Atijas, Baruh, Daniti, Danon, Eskenazi, Finci, Gaon, Kabiljo, Kajon, Kalderon, Kamhi, Katan, Konforti, Kunorti, Levi, Maestro, Montilja, Obadija, Ozmo, Pardo, Pesah, Pinto, Romano, Shalom, Toledano.

Sarajevo's Ashkenazim were smaller in number than the Sephardim. However their loyalty to God, Torah, the Jewish people and the land of Israel was profound and full of enthusiasm. So was their love for their fellowmen and Yugoslavia. Their patriotism was impeccable. The Ashkenazim of Sarajevo wrote a glorious chapter in the history of the city in less than a century of organized, communal existence. There was after the rise of Nazism a short lived movement among Yugoslavia's Ashkenazim to change their German sounding names by translating them into Serbo-Croatian. However the idea did not materialize. Only a few succeeded in doing so. Legal procedure was required. The Yugoslav bureaucracy in Belgrade was too slow. There were also sentimental reasons why not too many made an energetic effort. The author would like to pay homage to the Ashkenazim of Sarajevo with a quotation from the ancient Rabbis: "Whosoever gives permanence to the words of a deceased redeems his lips from the silence of the grave."

PART III
Destruction And Survival

Destruction And Survival

The thirtieth anniversary of the Warsaw Ghetto uprising (27 Nisan 5703-27 Nisan 5733) and the 25th anniversary of Israel's Independence (5 Iyar 5708-5 Iyar 5733) are reminders of the most terrible horror and greatest promise in Jewish history of the last two millenia.

The symbolism which links these two anniversaries is The Quest for Survival. For the Diaspora Jews and Israelis alike the need to understand the profound meaning of Jewish existence is to correlate history experienced by Jews in hostile Diaspora lands with history shaped in our ancient Homeland. The meaning and purpose of Jewish existence will be fortified everywhere by an objective and factual evaluation of what we know to be real facts about the plan and execution of the "Final Solution." It will enable us to understand the indestructible Hope for Survival, the unusual Will to Rise from the ruins and ashes of Slaughter as if "flying on eagles' wings." The creative Urge to build again, the compelling Drive "to run and not to be weary," (Isaiah 40, 31), which assume profound meaning that signifies uniqueness.

Pain and filth, degradation and suffering, could not extinguish the spark of hope. Horror and cruelty existed not only in the ghettos and concentration camps, but elsewhere in Europe, from the fjords of Norway to the shores of the Black Sea. Barbarism does not mean lack of brain or lack of human efficiency. The Nazis had these qualities and believed that the end justifies the means. Goebbels used to say: "Important is not what is right but what wins." Believing in this principle, Germany entered the War. World War II represented—generally speaking—the highest number of casualties in the history of mankind. When the Russians overran the concentration camps in Poland they found enough Zyklon B to gas 20 million people. It indicated that the Nazis had plans to gas non-Germanic people as well, not only Jews. After all there were only 3 million Jews left in Europe. The chilling reality is that the Germans meant what they preached. The Western world, the rest of humanity, did not comprehend, or did not want to understand, what was happening.

There is ample evidence that even Hitler was not omnipotent. He compromised when he saw that he could not have everything his own way, and realized that the German people would not follow him. The attempt to establish a German-Christian Church under Reich-Bishop Ludwig Mueller was met with spontaneous mass resistance, and the idea was ultimately dropped. The Nazi-inspired German-Christian Faith Movement led by Hitler's Army Chaplain Mueller, who was the Fuehrer's Plenipotentiary for the affairs of the Evangelical Church, was short lived. Mueller was unable to either appease or crush the opposition against the attempts of "de-Judaization" of Christianity.

As early as 1920 the Protestant theologian Adolph von Harnack, who was not in the least an anti-Semite, thought that the greater part of Scripture, with the exception of the Prophets and Psalms, hindered the development of Christianity. He called the retention of the Old Testament as a canonical document in Protestantism, an "ecclesiastical paralysis." Mueller's ideas coincided with Harnack's, although his motivation was racial and not religious. Harnack's idea represented action by spiritual means and not by violence and terror. The leaders of Protestantism in Hitler's Germany knew that Mueller's endeavor was the first step in the direction of "Neo-paganism." The Hitler-Rosenberg-Goebbels-Mueller attempt found vigorous opposition, and the idea of a "German Church under the sign of a Volk-myth" was terminated. The outbreak of War in 1939 mitigated the conflict between Protestantism and Nazism, which had lasted for several years.

The second example of Hitler's retreat was the attempt to promulgate the "Prevention of Progeny with Hereditary Disease." This law introduced in 1933, sanctioned euthanasia. Obsessed and preoccupied with racial superiority, the Nazis intended to eliminate all citizens who were racially and socially undesirable. The program called for the elimination of the insane, the incurables, shortly, of "valueless life." Euthanasia was reserved for Aryan Germans, and "asocials" of all nationalities. The German people appealed to their courts. The rank and file of German clergymen delivered fiery sermons against this practice. Ashes of cremated children, parents and relatives, which were sent to their families, aroused indignation and protest among the Germans. They became aware of a simple fact. The Nazis were serious in implementing the plan. Public opinion forced Hitler to scrap the euthanasia program. Whispers of protest rose to a clamor and proved to be effective. The program was discontinued in August, 1941. Once again the organized attitude and will of the German people prevailed, although the implementation of the program was practiced quietly and without fanfare.

The "Final Solution," too, was organized quietly and without noise. But there is one basic difference as far as the reaction of the German people is concerned. In the case of euthanasia, the lives of German nationals were at stake and the outcry was heard in Berlin and Berchtesgaden, in the churches and coffeehouses. In the case of crematoria where Jews, foreign laborers, Slavs, and anti-Nazis were burned, the German people were, conveniently, silent.

The "secrecy" of the crematoria was far from being a complete secret. It is true, it was not discussed publicly, but rather privately. Albert Speer had a friend who told him about a crematorium located in Silesia. Ten thousands of men and women like Speer had friends who let them in on the "secret" of other crematoria. Thousands of young women worked as telephone operators, "Blitzgirls," and shared the secret with their families. European peoples, not only the governments, knew that crematoria existed. European governments-in-exile warned their nations to be aware of the German menace. The Western World, the Allies, were kept informed, repeatedly, about the atrocities. Only those who did not want to know were unaware of the existence of crematoria. Only those among the Germans who did not care, did not notice that thousands of Jews and many of their Christian neighbors disappeared.

Great and small nations of the pagan world had been more "civilized" as conquerers than the Germans. The Jews faced many hostile nations in their long history of almost four thousand years. The Babylonians caused destruction and presented the first challenge to Jewish survival. However the peril was met resolutely, with new ideas, and the Jews prevailed in spite of the exile. As a rule nations do not survive dispersion. Although they were a small, subjugated people, forcibly exiled to a distant land, the Jews did not disintegrate. After two generations the exiles returned to their homeland. Their national identity and religious life was strengthened. They were a reborn people. They continued life as a people in the land of their fathers.

The Greco-Roman period brought challenge to Jewish survival for the second time. Hellenism represented danger of assimilation through Greek art, philosophy and literature. The Roman legions represented annihilation because Rome had the most powerful and best equipped army. The Jews were able to survive. The book replaced the sword. The soldier became a student of the Torah.

The Diaspora lasted for almost nineteen hundred years. The Jews came in contact with nations and civilizations throughout the world and survived as a distinct people. The loss of human lives was enormous. The challenge to survival was persistent on all continents and in all climates. The Jews were forced to cross oceans and mountains, but they did not journey empty-handed. They carried with them the Scroll of the Torah. They called attention of Christian and Islamic peoples to the Decalogue. The bush burned many times, but was never consumed. There were times when survival was very difficult. However the hope for a miracle sustained the nation in time of crisis.

Miracles of survival are as much a part of Jewish history as Hebrew is a part of Jewish identity and culture. Challenge to Jewish survival is an old phenomenon. Although conquerors as well as "hospitable" nations treated subjugated peoples and alien minorities harshly, the Jews survived nevertheless. Their faith in a better future and hope to return to their ancient homeland kept them alive.

During this long period of Jewish history the challenge to survive was real, but did not pose a threat of complete *physical* annihilation. Rome governed the Jews with an iron fist, but did not insist upon the total destruction of the Jewish People. The idea of the "Final Solution" was conceived and planned in the twentieth century. It was contrived on January 20, 1942, at the fashionable suburb of Berlin, which became known as the "Wansee conference." The idea of annihilating the Jews was affirmed as the dogma and top priority of Nazi Warfare.[20]

The Holocaust is a part of Jewish as well as of human history. A Jewish child in Los Angeles or a German child in Bonn, a Czech child in Lidice or a Dutch child in Amsterdam, and an Israeli child in Jerusalem, have one thing in common, curiosity. They want to know what happened in the years 1933-1945. A society without curiosity about the past will have little to contribute to the future. Buber had stated that "we Jews are a community based on memory. A common memory has kept us together and enabled us to survive."[21] To understand the Holocaust fully is mandatory not only to a Jew, but to the rest of mankind as well.

Humans capable of rational thinking and expressing feelings cannot easily dismiss an experience which contains a key to understanding ourselves, our time and its place in history. Theologians and moralists, political and social scientists, psychologists and psychiatrists should be advised to study the Holocaust as a part of their specialized fields. To the best of our knowledge this idea has not been implemented. Even history departments at our schools of higher learning hesitate, after three decades, to probe into the meaning of the Holocaust.

I have been intrigued by oversimplifications, inaccuracies, and sometimes misrepresentations of history. How do "historic" inaccuracies come about? Historians are familiar with the story of Sir Walter Raleigh, the English historian and statesman, who lived

---

[20] Dieter Wisliceny's affidavit before the International Military Tribunal at Nurnberg, January 3, 1946, Nazi Conspiracy and Aggression, Washington 1946 v. viii, pp. 606-621.—Gerald Reitlinger, The Final Solution, 1953. Erich Goldhagen, Midstream, October, 1971.

[21] M. Buber, Israel and the World. Schocken Books, New York, 1948, p. 146.

a turbulent life four hundred years ago. While imprisoned in the Tower of London he heard a brawl in the courtyard. When he questioned several guardsmen about it, each of them described the brawl in a different way. Sir Walter, we are told, tore up the manuscript of his History of the Romans, exclaiming: "If I cannot find out what happened yesterday, how can I give a reliable account of what happened two thousand years ago?"

Inaccuracies and oversimplifications are phenomena of history. We Jews have been victimized and mulcted because of inaccurate records of history. This was often beyond our control. It took Christianity nineteen hundred years to exonerate the Jews of the guilt of the crucifixion of Jesus. The synoptic gospels (Matthew, Mark and Luke) differ from the gospel of John in their account as to the role and mood of the Jews under the Romans. The Governor of Judea, Pontius Pilate, governed the Jews with an iron fist at the time of the event described in the gospels. An arrogant and ruthless Roman emperor was represented in Judea by a governor equally ruthless and arrogant. The Quislings, who collaborated with the governor, were treated with scorn and disgust by the true Jewish patriots. The Pharisees and Sadducees, the priests and scribes, wanted to preserve Sanhedrin's authority and prevent Roman encroachment upon the Jewish nation. Whosoever witnessed the Nazis in action during World War II, not only in Norway and France but elsewhere, including Poland and the Ukraine, will understand what Roman oppression meant. The Jews had felt hurt and pain when another Jew, one of their sons, was being persecuted and victimized.

Hundreds of generations of Jews have been, since the time of the crucifixion, indiscriminately penalized for a crime which neither they nor their ancestors committed. Eminent scholars in our time (James Parkes, Samuel Sandmel, Jules Isaac, Robert L. Wilken, S.G.F. Brandon, William Riley Wilson, Haim H. Cohn) opened the door for the correction of history's greatest injustice. What we are witnessing today in ecumenism, should it lead to positive results, is the awakening of human conscience. We hope that man can be "educated" and prejudice can be transformed into enlightenment. To put it in a brief sentence written by Buber, "How delightful a thing a human being could be, if he were a human being."[22]   World War II, Pope John XXIII and the

---

[22] Buber, Ibidem, p. 242. Compare John Dewey, Problems of Men.

ecumenical movement brought the opportunity for a dialogue between Christians and Jews. The door has been opened and the Jewish People rightfully hope that history's painful distortion will be corrected eventually.

The Catholic News of June 10, 1971 printed the following statement by Rabbi Marc Tanenbaum: "Catholics and Jews share a universal agenda . . . building a human community between people who share a very great deal as brothers and sisters who inherit a common covenant. A feeling of confidence and trust, a sense of mutual helpfulness begins to develop." It is too early to rejoice and call ecumenism a success, and premature to dismiss it and describe it as a failure. It is a hopeful sign, characteristic of our time. The search to find answers to very difficult, almost unsolvable questions, is commendable. Should an alliance between Christian and Jews be established for the sole purpose of sensitizing and humanizing the world community, of building bridges based on mutual concern and trust, then it will help also to respect each other's particular principles, way of life and agenda for the future.

Jewish historiography presents us with a classical example of uncertainty, in the case of Josephus Flavius. Was he a committed Jew or a traitor, a Jewish patriot or a Roman spy? Jost, Graetz, Dubnov, Baron do not satisfy our curiosity.

Historiography has considerably changed since Josephus and Sir Walter Raleigh. Are modern historians always accurate? What causes "chronic" inaccuracy, even misrepresentation? I feel discomfort and anguish when the History of the Holocaust is presented inaccurately. Trustworthy methods of examining sources and the implementation of historiography are mandatory not only for the historian. They are as important in writing psycho-philosophical dissertations, religio-theological treatises and even documentary novels or poetry. One of the reasons why Holocaust history was not written according to the principles guiding historiography, lies in the fact that historians began to write about it "before the dust settled," before all sources dealing with the Nazi horror could be collected, published and researched. New publications appear all the time. Important material is still buried in archives and in private hands. Comprehensive studies are being published which will enable a contemporary Graetz, Dubnov or Baron to dedicate all his life to the analysis and writing of the Holocaust history. The state of shock after the War prevented many Jewish survivors from participating actively in the process of clarifying problems and questions about the horror of Destruction and Survival. Almost three decades after World War II, we are still far from being able to understand clearly the perpetrators and victims of the greatest horror ever committed. To broaden our outlook and dimensions, and to deepen our knowledge must be our task. The understanding of this tragic period by future generations depends upon it.

When conventional behavior breaks down, and physical instincts for survival triumph, when fear paralyzes nobility of the soul and undermines the sensitivity of the mind, then rare heroism reveals itself in its entire breadth and depth. In an institutionalized society, in peace time, sadism and bestiality are overshadowed by helpfulness and kindness. But when standard behavior and public opinion hardly exist, man's character generally finds expression in acts totally divorced from moral injunctions and ethical values. Acts of kindness and spiritual heroism, under those circumstances, prove that man and nature can rise up to God, even in time of crisis.

The Holocaust literature has a great message; the search for meaning of human existence. Discovering the other face of our age, not only its doubts, questions and perplexities about man's nature and his future, will help us to comprehend that humanity did not surrender and that the Nazis failed to impose their pattern upon European nations. The ideological germs of Nazism-Fascism did not destroy the basic human values. The literature of the Holocaust bears witness to that. While research is going on and new material and ideas are being published, it is important, at this point, that we re-evaluate the Holocaust literature.

I suggest that we re-examine the following four aspects of the Holocaust: 1) Historiography, 2) The Psycho-Philosophical Thought, 3) The Religio-Theological Aspect, and 4) Imaginative Literature.

1

Re-evaluation of

Holocaust Literature

The need to re-evaluate and re-examine the four aspects of the Holocaust Literature will be discussed in the following pages.

1. Historiography.

The literature of the Holocaust is relatively young. Nevertheless it has grown considerably. This much can be said: that since the late 1940s, and even since the 1950s, new material has been published. Many important books—some of them real classics—have been added to the bookshelves of the Holocaust library. And indeed a library it is; it encompasses thousands of volumes in many languages and genres. No single person can become fully familiar with this literature. Although a number of historians have made meaningful contributions to the understanding of the Destruction, the fact remains that Holocaust history is still awaiting its historian of the caliber of a Graetz, Dubnov or Baron. Great strides have been made and the material is being organized and prepared for such a historian.

The tragedy of the Holocaust is not only the most terrible chapter in Jewish history, but a human-universal catastrophe, raising all kinds of doubts and anxieties about the nature of man and the future of mankind. Furthermore the universal interest in the Holocaust is widespread and evidenced by the following fact. Jews and non-Jews have participated in writing and publishing of important material related to World War II; monographs, memoirs, diaries, and letters. Of course, these writings were not printed at the time when Gerald Reitlinger and Raul Hillberg wrote their otherwise excellent books, "The Final Solution" and "The Destruction of the European Jews."[23] They were acclaimed by other historians, among them H.R. Trevor-Roper, as their spokesmen. According to their thesis the Jewish "victims—caught in the strait jacket of their history—plunged themselves physically and psychologically into catastrophe. The destruction of the Jews was thus no accident."[24]

Galut mentality and Jewish reaction to tyranny during the last two thousand years broke down completely before the Nazi assault. Because of the absence of any resistance the Jewish community unwittingly contributed its share towards its own destruction. At least part of the responsibility is assigned to the Jewish victims of the Holocaust. Reitlinger, Hillberg and Trevor-Roper are in a sense responsible for introducing into the Holocaust history such terms as "Diaspora mentality," "Ghetto psychology," "Jewish behavior," and extreme "Jewish passivity," which allegedly characterized European Jews. Furthermore, according to the same thesis the Jews "collaborated" with the Nazis. This "collaboration" was not only a moral blemish but contributed to the process of extermination.

None of these three historians was familiar with Jewish sources, or was in a position to study books written in Yiddish, or the other languages of the occupied territories. Their knowledge of the socio-political structure of the Jewish Eastern European Community was negligent. They used exclusively German sources, meaning Nazi documentary material; they were totally unin-

---

[23] London, 1953, New York, 1954–Quandrangle Books, Chicago, 1961.

[24] Commentary, November, 1963, p. 369. Gerald Reitlinger, The Final Solution, London, 1953, New York, 1954. K. Shabbetai, As Sheep to the Slaughter, New York–Tel Aviv, 1963, p. 10.

formed about the reaction of Jewish groups to Nazism as exemplified by Bundists, Zionists, Revisionists and other groups. The American weekly Colliers published an article, in July 1944, and called it "The Great Contribution to the War by the Little Jewish People." The author of the article, Frank Gerwasi, stated that although Jews were fighting the Nazis as Allied soldiers and as partisans in the occupied countries the myth persists that the Jews are not fighters "but a nation of shopkeepers and bankers."

Dr. Yehezkel Lewin, the martyred Rabbi of Lwow, told me on August 25, 1939, in the presence of a friend, Dr. David Kahane, today Rabbi in Buenos Aires, that he had visited on that day the headquarters of the commanding general begging him to arm the Betarim (a Jewish paramilitary youth group of Revisionism), camping at Tatra Mountains, in the face of imminent German peril. Most of the Betarim had military training, many were reservists of the Polish Army and could be useful in defending Poland in case of a German Blitz. "Rabbi," answered the general, "if the glorious Polish Army cannot defend Poland we don't want your boys to be the defenders of the Polish nation."

The Betarim waited for the good news which was supposed to reach them but never did. They joined the ranks of victims rather than fighters; they waited hopefully for the opportunity which prejudice and shortsightedness denied them. The Betarim could have written a heroic page in the history of Poland. This was the time to organize Jewish manpower effectively. It was too late eighteen days later, too late for Poland and too late for the Jewish people.

My martyred brother was an attorney in a small town, Kozowa, Eastern Galicia, across the Soviet frontiers. He was hiding in the forests, with his wife and young daughter in winter 1942-43. A local farmer, an old friend of the family, fed them. His brother was the liaison between myself and my family, being interned in a Polish military camp at the Balaton, in Hungary. Ultimately the farmer and my brother joined the partisans; however my brother was not accepted till he could afford to buy and bring with him a rifle. He was advised to send back his wife and child to Kozowa, to live with Aryan friends. While it is true that it was possible to purchase a rifle it is also true that very few Jews could afford this kind of luxury and the help of a reliable Aryan friend. This rare combination of available means and willing friends did not occur too often.

This was not an isolated episode. Similar situations prevailed in other regions where Jews wanted to join partisans, particularly where Jewish units were to be formed. The number of men at the Narocz forest permitted the formation of such a unit. Isaac Kowalski's excellent book[25] tells the story of Jewish partisans of the Narocz forest, Northeastern Poland. Some five hundred Jewish partisans, poorly armed, came to the forest to join the "Voroshilov" battalions. They waited for the orders from Brigadier Fiodor Gregorowicz Markow, who commanded the Voroshilov battalions in the region. To their surprise "a group of heavily armed men led by Szaulewicz surrounded the unarmed Jewish partisans, forcing them at gun point to take off their good boots, leather jackets and hand them over. When the Jewish partisans began to grumble and complain to Markow, they were met with a cold shoulder. The Jews considered this episode as an act of anti-Semitism."

About this time Markow was visited by Major general Klimow, who flew in from Moscow. In 1940-41 Klimow was secretary of the Wilejka region, not far from Vilna and had a rank comparable to an American governor. He had come now to inspect the ranks of the Partisan Movement in White Russia. He called in the new Jewish partisans in order to get acquainted with them. In the course of his tour of inspection he remarked: "How come that so many of you lack weapons?" He continued: "And if you had no weapons why did you come into the forest?" Kowalski writes: "We of the Vilna ghetto were aware of the fact that the first condition of being accepted into any partisan unit was the possession of at least a revolver and bullets." He explains how in the ghetto the United Jewish Partisan Organization provided weapons for everybody. Once in the forest, under the command and jurisdiction of the Soviet military authority, this obligation and responsibility should have been met by the Red Army.

"All this depressed the Jews in the forest to a great extent. They waited stoically for a more propitious time which would be more favorable for the Jewish partisans who did not have any weapons." Nevertheless "Narocz forest produced a great amount of heroes. One partisan, Isaac Blatt, was post-mortem awarded the

---

[25] A secret Press in Nazi Europe, Central Guide Publishers, Inc., 1969, pp. 267-271.

highest title, Hero of the Soviet Union, for his tremendous courage."

New publications in the last couple of years,[26] among them books by Isaac Kowalski, Jacob Presser, Kazimierz Iranek-Osmecki, and Father Carlo Falconi[27] make re-evaluation of Holocaust historiography mandatory. Particularly Szajowski's Gazetteer is a sourcebook for future generations of the Catastrophe period. Although the general population of France was during this period Anti-Semitic, the Jews played an important role in the French resistance movement. French Jews actually started organized resistance, two of the three regional chiefs being Jews. Szajowski is also the first historian to demonstrate that the Jewish catastrophe in France actually began with the end of the Spanish Civil War. [28]

It was not till the 1960s that greater objectivity entered into the discussion led, partly, by those who experienced the Holocaust, and partly, by others who could not agree with a generalization which was felt to be an unfair oversimplification. Once "the dust settled," the official archives became available, and privately owned material began reaching the historian, the need for re-evaluation became evident. Men and women, who for years had suppressed their agonies, began to write and publish. This material is of great importance and will help the historian to employ principles of authenticity and historicity.

Jacob Presser's, "The Destruction of the Dutch Jews"[29] is a classic. It took Presser, a distinguished historian, eighteen years to research and analyze the available material. Although the book was commissioned by Netherlands State Institute of War Documentation for the year 1952 it was not till 1968 that the book was published. Presser has proven the point that unless "the dust has settled," the official archives have been made available and material by eyewitnesses has been examined, no historian can claim the right of having done justice to historiography. Presser's book presents a definitive account of the Holocaust in the

---

[26] Analytical Franco-Jewish Gazetteer, The American Academy of Jewish Research, New York, 1970.

[27] The Silence of Pius XII, Little, Brown and Company, 1970.

[28] The Reconstructionist, July 9, 1971, pp. 31-4.

[29] E.P. Dutton & Co., Inc., New York, 1969.

Netherlands. It was not written hastily, and used, in addition to Dutch sources, German documents as well.

Iranek-Osmecki's book, "He Who Saves One Life,"[30] is another valuable addition to Holocaust literature which proves again that it takes a quarter of a century till the dust settles. He is a military historian and former Colonel of the military staff of the Polish Government in exile, London, 1939-1945. Iranek is familiar with all aspects and facets of World War II as well as with every detail of the German occupation of Poland, which he visited as an emissary in 1941 and again in 1943. His book contains important and revealing material never before published. It tells the story of how the Polish Government abroad—and in Poland—tried to assist the oppressed Jews.

Iranek's book is well written, fairly organized, and meticulously documented. The author opens new vistas when he described diplomatic activities of the Polish Government in London in behalf of Poland's oppressed Jewry. The embassies in Washington and Rome were very active calling attention to and submitting proof of German atrocities. The Information Center in New York related actual information to the American leadership and to the public. The Polish Government in exile was not successful in mobilizing help of the Allies. The leaders of the free world did not want to be bothered with details of the horror. The Allies refused again and again to bomb the railroads leading to Auschwitz and other crematoria. The diplomatic efforts and interventions failed. The results of all interventions were practically nil. Edward Raczynski, Foreign Minister, demanded that appropriate measures be taken to stop further atrocities. He warned on December 17, 1942, during a B B C broadcast that if the Allies keep silent "the stones will cry out." The Polish Government in exile sounded the alarm that "the Jewish Community in Poland is doomed to extermination." The answer of the Allies was vague, noncommittal. The Allies defined their policy as follows: nothing must interfere with War efforts, help for the victims will be forthcoming as soon as possible, and the guilty will be punished after the War. Nevertheless the humanitarian efforts of the Polish Government stand up high.

[30]Crown Publishers, Inc., New York, 1971.

Mr. Papée, the Polish Ambassador to the Holy See was instructed to deliver letters to the Vatican. The Poles begged for help. The President of Poland in London, Wladyslaw Raczkiewicz, wrote to Pope Pius XII begging him to intervene: "I lay this prayer of the martyred nation at the feet of Your Holiness." But the prayer was not favorably received.[31]

Iranek published in his book authentic documents from the archives of the former Polish Government in exile. Archives of other Governments in exile are available. The American Government has declassified highly secret documents and the historian can easily obtain them. This material is essential to historiography as much as were the German files and documents captured in 1945. It permits us to see the other side of the coin and to understand the tragedy more objectively.

Declassified secret wartime correspondence between President Franklin D. Roosevelt and Winston Churchill, archived in the Roosevelt Library at Hyde Park, provides fresh insight into the relationship of Roosevelt to the Jewish problem and the Zionist cause during the days of World War II. Conflicting with the widely held belief that Roosevelt was a friend of the Jewish people and a champion of the Zionist cause, is a secret memorandum of the conversation on the Palestine question that took place between Roosevelt and King Ibn Saud abroad the U.S. Destroyer Quincy on February 14, 1945, immediately following the Yalta meeting with Churchill and Stalin. The memorandum begins: "The President asked his Majesty (Ibn Saud) for his advice regarding the problem of Jewish refugees driven from their homes in Europe. His Majesty replied that, in his opinion, the Jews should return to live in the lands from which they were driven." In response the President remarked that Poland might be considered as a case in point. "The Germans appear to have killed three million Polish Jews, by which acccunt there should be space in Poland for the resettlement of many homeless Jews," Roosevelt said. (New York, ZINS, B'nai B'rith Messenger, June 30, 1972).

In an age of persisting crisis yesterday's horror is fading away. It is for that reason that books such as "While Six Million Died," by Arthur D. Morse[32] and "The Politics of Rescue,—The Roosevelt

---

[31] Jewish Spectator, March, 1972, p. 19.

[32] Random House, New York, 1968.

Administration and the Holocaust, 1938-1945," by Henry L. Feingold[33] are being hardly noticed. A generation that has difficulties in digesting its own failures will display limited empathy for the shocking experience of its predecessors. This lapse of American conscience, tragic and discouraging, is an indictment of the generation which watched but did nothing to halt the greatest mass murder in modern history.

Rabbi Abba Hillel Silver and Hayim Greenberg, the eloquent spokesmen of American Jewry, anticipated Morse's and Feingold's verdict. When Silver addressed an assemblage in New York City, twenty-seven years ago, he stated: "The great democracies heard the tortured cry of a dying people. They wagged their heads in sympathy and then proceeded to speak in barren legalism of constricted hearts of their inability to intervene in the domestic affairs of other nations and of their own inviolate immigration laws."[34] Morse's and Feingold's works, to mention only two new publications, are based on authentic documents of the American archives; they would normally arouse guilt feelings in the minds of responsible leaders for opportunities they overlooked. It would be too much to expect our troubled generation to shed tears because millions have perished during those ghastly years, who could have been saved. Hayim Greenberg published an article on February 12, 1943, in Yiddisher Kempfer, entitled "Bankrupt" in which he condemned American Jews because in their majority they had either limited themselves to expressing sorrow or had been preoccupied with factional disputes. He wanted to arouse American public opinion while apathy and passivity characterized American Jewish organizations.[35]

We are grateful to Morse and Feingold for another reason. They brought into the open the abortive and clumsy role played by the International Red Cross. Strangely enough the I.R.C. failed dismally in its mission of humanitarianism during the Axis fury. A comprehensive study of this vital, international agency, covering all occupied countries is badly missing. We must learn from its failures and shortcomings or we won't be able to improve the status of the International Red Cross.

---

[33] Rutgers University Press, New Brunswick, New Jersey, 1970.

[34] Midstream, May, 1968, p. 72.

[35] Midstream, Ibidem, p. 62.

The attitude of the I.R.C. was nebulous, noncommittal and vague. Claiming that it held no sanction to meliorate the plight of persecuted minorities it encouraged Nazi aggressiveness. The excuse of its indifference was that intervention on behalf of oppressed minorities might jeopardize the effectiveness of its cardinal task, mainly the supervision and care of POW's. For no reason whatsoever its leaders even accepted the degrading Nazi identification of Jews as "stateless persons" or "common criminals" and only after the Allied victory was a certainty did the organization lend a hand at salvaging the remnant of European Jewry.[36]

It should be recalled in this connection, that when the Red Cross Committee proposed, after the declaration of war in 1939, that the belligerents extend the benefits of the Geneva Convention to the civil populations, "without distinction of race, religion or politics," it was—by a cruel paradox and lack of foresight—that Great Britain had showed the most reluctance, while the Third Reich "declared itself ready to discuss the project." Even if it had been accepted, nothing would have kept the Nazis from disregarding it. But the question would then have had a different basis, and the Red Cross, the neutrals, and the Allies would have been in a better position to do something. The fact that the Jewish prisoners of war were never touched by the Nazis is very significant and speaks for itself.

In a circular letter dated September 4, 1939, the International Committee of the Red Cross proposed to the belligerents, among other measures, "the anticipated and at least provisional adoption, only for the present conflict and for its duration, of the provisions of the above-mentioned proposed convention." (This referred to the so-called Tokyo project, which extended to civilians the benefits of the Geneva Convention.)[37]

In a letter dated November 30, 1939, the Reich Ministry of Foreign Affairs confirmed that "on the German side, it is believed that the Tokyo project can serve as the basis for concluding an international agreement on the treatment and protection of civilians in enemy or occupied territory."

[36] Midstream, Ibidem, p. 67.

[37] Harvest of Hate, pp. 259-260.

On November 23, 1939, the government of the Third Republic wrote: "The French government fully recognizes the interest . . . of the so-called Tokyo project. It believes, however, that the text in question requires careful study . . . that might entail a fairly long delay and postpone the solution of the problems."

As for the British government, only on April 30, 1940, did it answer the circular letter, indicating that it preferred to make a bilateral agreement with the government of the Third Reich.

The Feingold findings concerning the International Committee of the Red Cross (ICRC) are revealing. "The ICRC was reluctant to extend its food parcel service to camps, claiming that it had no authority except through whatever good will individual belligerents might show. Nor did it have enough funds. Nahum Goldman requested government fundings on September 16, 1943. In November, the Department decided to honor the request at least nominally by granting the ICRC four million dollars. But such funds were not extended to the ICRC until August, 1944. A host of new problems arose to block implementation of the program."[38]

While the ICRC remained hesitant because of its fear of offending Berlin, Breckinridge Long saw to it that the State Department should not act hastily. The American and British Red Cross standard parcels were reserved for civilian internees and prisoners of War. Segregated Jews did not belong to either of two categories, according to the German definition. The Holocaust was a part of insanity and madness of World War II. Among the world leaders were some who had the foresight to comprehend that Auschwitz was a separate tragedy. Unfortunately they represented the governments in exile and had very little to say in these matters. The role that the American Jewish Community played was very difficult. Furthermore there was no unity among the different groups within the Jewish Community. A man who was as difficult and harsh as Long realized the weakness of the Jewish situation. A community which needed to speak to Roosevelt with one voice remained disunited and fragmentized. "Disunity and powerlessness were characteristic of Jewish communities everywhere and the United States was no exception."[39]

[38]The Politics of Rescue, Ibidem, pp. 188-9.

[39]The Politics . . . Ibidem, p. 299.

The activity of the Volksbund and the role which it played during the crucial years 1939-1945 is waiting to be researched and written. The deportation of Jewish communities from Central Europe to concentration camps would be better comprehended. While the headquarters of the Volksbund were in Berlin its communication lines were connected with the Baltic and Northern regions as well as Central Europe. In each occupied country the Volksbund assisted the Wehrmacht in many ways: in providing lists of the opposition leaders, Jews and leftists; recruitment of young men from the ranks of the German ethnic group into the active service of the German army; the collection of raw material, which was badly needed in Germany; establishing contacts with Volksbund leaders in distant places, etc. Nazi agents penetrated the German ethnic minorities wherever they resided. They were able to influence the thinking of Volga Germans who were far away.

All this, and the knowledge of many other facts still waiting to be researched, can help us to answer the crucial question: "What exactly did happen and how did it happen?" The historian who writes a book about the Holocaust but does not know all that can be known, is doing a disservice to historiography. Never before in modern history has a major power been defeated without destroying its archives. Even leading Nazis, among them Goebbels, left their diaries to the victors. While this permitted the scholars to probe hastily into the best guarded secrets of Nazism, it also proved to be a disadvantage from the point of view of historicity. It limited research and was responsible for jumping hastily to conclusions.

The dust has still not settled on the heated controversy about the silence of the Churches in general and the Vatican in particular during World War II. The tragic history of the Nazi era reveals that major organized religions were the only communities within the broader structure of German society which could have successfully helped to withstand the regime's attempt to achieve a perfect totalitarian order. We are grateful to Gordon C. Zahn, "German Catholics and Hitler's War: A Study of Social Control,"[40] and Arthur C. Cochrane, "The Church's Confession under Hitler,"[41]

[40] Sheed and Ward, New York, 1962.

[41] Westminster, Philadelphia, 1962.

for their studies. Even those Catholic "bishops who displayed heroic resistance of Nazi attacks upon Christianity and the Church—Von Gallen, Faulhaber and Groeber—openly and wholeheartedly supported Hitler's wars of ruthless aggression while criticial of the neopaganism of National Socialism."[42] Protestant leaders on the other hand saw clearly the conflict between "the true and the false Church" but "the men responsible for its heroic challenge were sufficiently imbued with the nationalistic spirit to enable them to avoid taking a stand against a series of patently unjust wars."[43]

What could the Jews of Germany and Europe expect from Germany's spiritual leadership under such circumstances?

The Jewish Historical Museum in Amsterdam has an enlarged photograph which in a sense symbolizes how Jews feel about Christianity's role in the "Final Solution." The picture was taken in the famous concentration camp at Westerbork, Netherlands, at a Christmas party celebrated by S.S. and their women. Those who planned extermination and murdered the Jews were men and women whose exposure to religion was derived from Christian sources. Historians underline the fact that many of them were men with university education and professional training. In some instances even former pastors were active leaders of the work. At the end of November, 1944, the Gestapo liquidated its barracks in Buda, which were located at St. Imre-Hercog ut. We lived across the barracks in a house which carried a Swedish State emblem and a sign that it belonged to the Swedish Embassy. Next to the Swedish house was the office of a Hungarian dentist, whom Gestapo officers would visit as patients. Waiting patients, including the Gestapo men, would often become involved in a conversation. Jews who lived as disguised Aryans could not help but wonder how one and the same man could be a beast while on "duty," a gentle, almost sentimental man while talking about his own family. J. Presser explains it: "Many of the murderers were thugs and illiterates, but others were educated men with an undeniable love of literature, art and music; many were good family men, not without sensibility; most of them celebrated Christmas, taking time off from the massacre of their fellow-creatures." William

[42] Judaism, Spring, 1963, p. 244.
[43] Judaism, Ibidem, p. 243.

James coined the phrase "split-off-consciousness" describing the phenomenon of multiple personality.[44] They had no difficulty whatsoever in being loyal to Hitler and God at the same time.

Christian thinkers believe that Nazism was an anti-Christian explosion. This is undeniably true. Richard L. Rubenstein described a conversation with Dr. Heinrich Gruber, in summer 1961, Dean of the Evangelical Church in Berlin. Dean Gruber, a fiery anti-Nazi, whom Eichmann reprimanded for helping Jews and who spent some time in Dachau, was asked by Rubenstein whether he believed that it was God's will that Hitler should destroy the Jews? Dr. Gruber replied with a quotation from Psalms 44, 23: "For Thy sake we are slaughtered everyday." To him, Hitler was simply another rod, an instrument of God.[45] There is very little indication that this kind of mentality can be eradicated. Even genuinely decent people wrapped in metaphysical ideology have a long way to go before they can see facts of day to day living. There is an infinite quantity of pain in this realization. In spite of it the Protestant-Jewish dialogue must go on. Neither the Protestant nor the Jew can avoid it.

What is true of Protestant Churches is equally true of the Roman Catholic Church in Germany, and of the Vatican, representing Catholicism everywhere. The Catholic-Jewish dialogue is an ongoing program, and the 1970's are more promising than the previous decades were.

The following exchange of letters speaks for itself.

I see rays of hope in Father Morley's excellent review of Carlo Falconi's treatise, "The Silence of Pius XII."[46] I stated in a letter to him that "Catholic historians are still grappling with the dilemma of writing Papal history critically, based on principles of historiography. Their undivided loyalty to their faith, which the Pope represents regardless of the Pontiff's human failings, should be admired and respected. This attitude, however, will often hamper the results of the historic inquiry.

"Falconi admits that the Nazi approach to the Vatican was one of caution. The Nazi threats against the Catholic Church may have

---

[44] Jewish Spectator, January, 1971, p. 27.

[45] The Reconstructionist, October 19, 1962, p. 16.

[46] The Jewish Spectator, May, 1971, pp. 7-9.

been blackmail rather than a real menace! This statement makes it even more difficult to explain why Pope Pius XII did not adopt a decisive position. He knew of the Nazi atrocities and was appraised of them. Consequently, when the Pope remained silent, it was not because he was cautious and wanted to avoid Nazi reprisals against the Catholic Church in Germany or in German-occupied Europe, but rather because of his Germanophile attitude and disinterestedness in Jewish suffering. Lack of concern for Catholics in Poland in spite of urgent appeals made to the Vatican by the Polish Government in London, and through other channels, should have been another reason for Papal action on behalf of the persecuted. How can one speak under these circumstances of the Pope's 'honesty and good intentions'?

"That the book entails very little related to the Pope's silence vis-à-vis the Jews is understandable. There is very little that can be said about something he persistently ignored; it was, regrettably, of little concern to him. The Pope's attitude and lack of concern for the Jewish tragedy was evident in the offices of Papal Nuncios, which I visited in Zagreb as well as in Budapest.

"It is rather interesting to note that neither Falconi nor Morley raised the question of whether another Pope would have acted differently and condemned the Germans. (The condemnation by Pope Paul VI of the action of the United States in 1945 in dropping an atomic bomb on Hiroshima.[47]) It is gratifying to see Catholic historians writing today more objectively about Pope Pius XII than in the 1950's and 1960's."

Reverend John F. Morley replied, stating among other things; "I found your remarks both interesting and personally rewarding. Please permit me this opportunity to say a few more things. I am willing to admit the possibility of a 'complicated predicament' for the Catholic historian in regard to Pope Pius XII, but it does not seem to me that the historian who happens to be Catholic is affected by the same 'predicament'.

"The Germanophile attitude of the Pope is brought out by Falconi. I suspect, as you have mentioned, that its effects may have been far more extensive than hitherto admitted. Speculation as to how another Pope would have acted is tremendously engaging. I frankly do not think that Pius XI or Paul VI would

[47]New York Times, August 9, 1965, pp. 1-2.

have acted substantially differently. More than likely, however, John XXIII might have acted more forcefully. The fact that Paul VI condemned the atomic bombing by the United States is news to me, and, even if published in the Times, seems incredible. I will have to research it further.

"I was happy to read your letter and enlightened by your comments, in particular, of course, the relating of your personal experience."

In my reply to Father Morley, I stated the following facts: "I trust that your busy schedule will permit you to continue this dialogue in the future.

"I am both impressed and enriched by my contacts, past and present, with Catholic priests and laymen. Carlo Falconi's treatise and your book review were used to underline the change which took place. What was impossible in the 1950s and 1960s became reality in 1971. This change opens the road to historiography.

"Permit me to make two additional points. Firstly; the agonizing experience, called Holocaust, entails very painful moments. As a Jew and Rabbi I don't hide my agony whenever I discuss the Jewish Police in the ghettos. 'Bitterly hated by their fellow Jews the members of the Jewish Police wrote a black page. That page cannot be torn out of the history books. That is impossible. If we try to do it—we shall not learn much that way.'[48]

"Secondly; my personal experience during World War II brought me in very close contact with leading Catholics. Alexander Akshamovich was Bishop of a diocese in Croatia, (Yugoslavia) where I started my calling as a Rabbi. He resided in Djakovo. In the Bishop's former flour-mill "Cereale" were concentrated 1,830 Jewish women and children, and 50 Serbian girls from Sarajevo, in December 1941. Akshamovich was my pupil—modern Hebrew—and friend. He was much older than myself. I visited the camp and saw the Bishop occasionally during the crucial winter of 1941-2.

"We shed tears together lamenting about the new situation which we were facing. The Bishop complained because his diocese was cut in two; one half remained in the 'Independent State of Croatia' while the second half was occupied by Hungary, causing

---

[48] Joseph Kermisz, The Place of the Ghetto Revolts in the Struggle against the Occupier, Reprinted from Jewish Resistance during the Holocaust, Yad Vashem, Jerusalem, 1970, p. 305.

not only administrative but also pastoral difficulties. I on the other hand was concerned with physical survival of the Jewish victims.

"I resided in Budapest after February, 1942 until the end of the war and came in close contact with a Polish Jesuit, Father Zbigniew, who was active in behalf of Poland since September, 1939. He introduced me to the Papal Nuncio in Budapest, Monsignior Angelo Rotta. The office of Monsignor Rotta was located at the Danube-promenade, overlooking the blue river and hills of Buda. The Nuncio was courteous, noncommittal and disinterested in the plight of the Jews. It was not until July 1944 that his attitude changed when deportations in Hungary reached their peak. The Vatican joined other neutrals: Sweden, Switzerland, Portugal and Spain, and opened a 'protective house' giving shelter to primarily converted Jews.

"Father Zbigniew and I had a great deal in common; we were Polish citizens and knew first hand what was going on in Poland and other countries. We both felt the anguish, pain and sorrow of Jeremiah. Father Zbigniew's heartache was caused by the suffering of the Poles and my pain was due to the distress of the Jews."

"On June 12, 1942 Marshal Pétain asked the French Ambassador to the Vatican, Bérard, to find out how the Pope felt about Vichy's Anti-Semitic statute on the Jews of June 3, 1941. Bérard reported back that the Pope had no criticism of this statute. Later on Vichy was able to claim that the Vatican had not objected to its Anti-Semitic policies.

"If we could agree on the principle that greatness and piety are relative while truth is absolute and should not be watered down for anybody's sake then you and I could make a small contribution to a better future of mankind. Father Zbigniew was aware of the fact that Pope Pius XII knew the truth about Poland, ignored the plight of his faithful pastors and the plea of his loyal followers. Recently the Vatican issued, among other things, a condemnation of the War in South East Asia. Not only did Pétain wait for encouragement from the Vatican but millions of Christians everywhere. Assuming that the Pope's intervention would not have helped, his empathy would have worked like a balm to the suffering and dying.

"I see hopeful signs indicating that a Catholic and Jewish historian could be fruitfully engaged in research of Holocaust history without encountering difficulties despite their separate loyalties. I am looking forward to such a day, when many-sided discussions will be conducted in the service of truth."

I wrote in 1964:[49] "When we left Paris for the United States in June, 1948, we brought with us cases of papers and documents relating to the Holocaust. It was in Stephen S. Wise's office, at the end of July, 1948, that I argued in his presence with two distinguished gentlemen—one affiliated with the World Jewish Congress, the other a well known Rabbi—that it was time to write the history of the Great Catastrophe. The longer we wait, I said, the more time and circumstances distort the facts of this tragic chapter. Lack of funds, hungry Jews in Europe, the needs of Israel and rebuilding Jewish lives were more important than the writing of history, argued the first. The second discussant remarked that YIVO is collecting material and doing research and a new chair in history dedicated to martyrdom at one of the leading Seminaries would be impossible."

A large literature has grown out of the Holocaust. However, there is lack of coordination. Hundreds and thousands of important documents were lost. Yad-Vashem was organized eight years after the Holocaust. The Eichmann trial helped to stir up emotions but did not help to clarify the issues. In the meantime, children in Israeli schools—and some of our youngsters—are asking, "Were the six million Jews really martyrs?" An Israeli Quarterly (State and Nation, Autumn 5723) complained about the "superficial treatment of the European Tragedy in Israeli schools. There are memorial ceremonies and occasional talks, but little systematic study. One reason for this is that most of the teachers have themselves but a perfunctory knowledge of the subject."

If this is true of Israel, what can we expect of our teachers? Our reading public has been greatly confused. Our Jewish periodicals— with some exceptions—either ignored the Holocaust or they conveyed shallow information. It is certainly gratifying to read in the Bulletin of the Jewish Theological Seminary of America[50] that Jewish college students, from diverse backgrounds, converged upon the Seminary this summer, and enrolled in a course of Holocaust as History. "Several students spoke of their need to

[49]The Jewish Spectator, January, 1964, pp. 10-11.

[50]August 1972, p. 1.

understand—e.g. the Holocaust—with emphasis upon how such a thing could have happened, and whether it could happen again. Can such questions be answered today, either by historians or by those who remember, or will it require another generation or more to acquire the perspective necessary to interpret this most traumatic of human experiences?" Non-Jewish institutions of higher learning have shown great interest in the study of the Holocaust. California State University, Fullerton, is among them.

The renowned historian, H. Ranke stated: "The Jews are the most historical of all nations." We must be aware of this title. It is our duty to research every page of this painful and tragic chapter known as Holocaust, Hoorban (Destruction) and Shoah (Desolation).

The Psycho-Philosophical Thought

Bruno Bettelheim needs no introduction. He is a recognized authority in the field of psychiatry and a well-known author of many learned books and articles. Alexander Donat, writer on the Holocaust, a survivor of the Warsaw Ghetto and of Nazi concentration camps, called Bettelheim's statements concerning the Holocaust, "the tasteless assault on the memory of the six million Jewish victims of the Nazi terror."[51] As one studies Bettelheim's articles, foreword to a book written by another psychiatrist and his own book concerning the catastrophe,[52] one cannot help but wonder how a great mind can be so dogmatic. Bettelheim repeats his own theory again and again, the way a pious Jew repeats the Sh'ma (Hear, oh Israel).

He wants us to believe that there is nothing that could or should be corrected, or added to the discussion of the Holocaust and the way he interprets it. There is nothing new, written lately, that could be said to influence his thinking. What had to be said was already said, by Bruno Bettelheim.

Professor Bettelheim was challenged by many. Among them were his own colleagues, prominent psychiatrists. One of them is

---

[51] Judaism, Fall 1963, p. 416.

[52] "Returning to Dachau," Commentary, February 1956–"The Ignored Lesson of Anne Frank," Harper's November 1960–"Auschwitz, A Doctor's Eyewitness Account," by Miklos Nyiszli, New York, 1960–"The Informed Heart," New York, 1961–"Arendt on Eichmann," The New Republic, June 16, 1963.

Victor E. Frankl, whose experience, first-hand knowledge and prominence in the field of psychiatry, cannot be overshadowed by anyone. The founder of Logotherapy, the third Viennese school of psychotherapy, challenged Bettelheim indirectly. Frankl's books concerning the extermination camps are discussed in this book in the essay "God and the Holocaust." Bettelheim decided to ignore facts unknown to him which were brought to his attention by historians, political scientists, sociologists and others. What is surprising is the fact that he reacted the same way to the challenge which came from fellow psychologists.

Judging by reports, Bettelheim continues the discussion on the Holocaust with survivors at the Chicago Psychoanalytic Society. Here, too, the purpose of the discussion is to prove that Jewish cowardice and passivity played directly into the hands of the Nazis, who welcomed this kind of cooperation. A "mutual identification" myth, identification with the aggressor, is the result of such an interpretation. "The impression is created that these survivors blame themselves for having failed in their duty as allies of the Nazis, an absurdity which was picked up by the New Left."[53]

The Bettelheim-Reitlinger-Hilberg-Arendt writings introduced a special terminology into their books and into the discussion of the Holocaust. Their method of psychoanalytical and socio-historical explanations caught on, at least at the beginning. The following "myths" were introduced: the "myth of cowardice," the "myth of life as usual," the "myth of collaboration" and the "myth of identification with the aggressor."

At one of the sessions of the Psychoanalytical Society in Chicago, Ernest A. Rappaport, Professor of Psychiatry, and a survivor of the Holocaust, volunteered to answer Bettelheim's question, directed to a patient-survivor, "Why were you spared?" Rappaport answered: "I was spared for not allowing myself to forget and maybe for not letting people whom I can reach forget."[54] The criticism directed at Dr. Bettelheim is not the result of his psychoanalytical attempt but rather because of over-simplifications. His writings are full of them.

[53] Ernest A. Rappaport, Midstream, August-September, 1971, p. 46.

[54] Midstream, Ibidem, p. 46.

Bettelheim follows Freud's pessimism concerning our age and civilization. It has been pointed out that according to Freud's teachings, the very nature of man is amoral. It leaves no hope that man at some time will behave according to the spirit of genuine moral values. "Freud insisted that human life is one long struggle against what he called the death instinct, and that we must keep these destructive strivings within bounds lest they send us to destruction. The twentieth century did away with ancient barriers that once prevented our destructive tendencies from running rampant, both in ourselves and in society. So their power to restrain or channel our destructive tendencies was weakened."[55] The old means of controlling the death instinct are obsolete and the new means of higher morality have not yet been achieved, so that very little is left to restrain man's destructive tendencies. Only man's personal ability to control his own death instinct can protect him when the destructive forces of others run rampant.

The Germans exterminated millions of people, Jews and non-Jews alike. Of the eleven million who were cremated, six million were Jews. "What was new, unique, terrifying, was that millions, like lemmings, marched themselves to their own deaths. This is what is incredible; this we must come to understand."[56] It is indeed regrettable that Bettelheim never heard of "the sanctification of Life," "kiddush ha-hayim." The late Rabbi Isaac Nissenbaum, one of the leaders of Poland's Jewry, in the Warsaw Ghetto during 1940-41, is credited with the following statement: "This is a time for kiddush ha-hayim, the sanctification of life, and not for kiddush ha-shem, the holiness of martyrdom. Previously the Jew's enemy sought his soul and the Jew sacrificed his body in martyrdom (i.e. he made a point of preserving what the enemy wished to take from him); now the oppressor demands the Jew's body and the Jew is obliged therefore to defend it, to preserve his life."[57]

The main reason, according to Bettelheim, why the Jews were unable to control their own "death instinct" and therefore walked themselves into the gas chambers, was their attitude. They continued "life as usual," "business as usual." Instead of risking

---

[55] Foreword to "Auschwitz, . . ." p. viii.

[56] Foreword to "Auschwitz, . . ." p. vii.

[57] Shaul Esh, Judaism, Spring, 1962, p. 106.

life, they lacked courage to risk action and permitted their death tendencies to flood them. It was this kind of "inertia" that led millions of Jews into the ghettos and hundred of thousands of Jews to sit home, waiting for their executioners. Those who did not allow inertia to take over, used the time wisely "to go underground, join resistance movements, provide themselves with forged papers, etc., if they had not done so long ago. Most of them survived."[58]

Bettelheim states this is what Jews should have done, but failed to do. They should have gone underground, they should have joined resistance movements, they should have provided themselves with forged papers. Why had they not done it? Let us take as an example German Jewish internees who were brought into Buchenwald in the fall of 1938. Bettelheim had an opportunity to talk to them, hundreds of them. "I asked them why they had not left Germany because of the utterly degrading and discriminating conditions they were subjected to. Their answer was: 'How could we leave? It would have meant giving up our homes, our places of business.' Their earthly possessions had so taken possession of them that they could not move; instead of using them, they were run by them."[59] If in spite of Nazi Party pressure and well-organized boycotts, Jewish shopkeepers managed to stay in business until 1938, then this condition changed rapidly in the Fall of 1938. The erosion of citizenship rights and other measures against the Jews were too obvious and insidious in nature to leave any hope of staying in Germany. If German Jews were not leaving by the ten thousands, then the reason for it was that they had no place to go.

What actually happened in Fall of 1938 was the assassination of Von Rath, Chancellor of the embassy in Paris, by Hershel Gruenspan. This led to the "Crystal Night" pogrom and destruction of synagogues, shops and flats, on November 9-10, 1938. Two days later decrees were issued concerning elimination of German Jews from the economy and payment of a collective fine of 125 thousand million marks. Ultimately on December 3, 1938 the decree was issued concerning immediate compulsory Aryanization of all Jewish enterprises and shops. It is a well-known fact that by

[58] Foreword, Ibidem, p. x.
[59] Foreword, Ibidem, p. xi.

December, 1938 even Jewish babies in Germany knew that there was no future for them in Hitler's Reich.

To describe the socio-economic situation of German Jewry in the Fall of 1938 as one based on a "business-as-usual" attitude and of self-delusion is an oversimplification. It is the same kind of reasoning which permits Bettelheim to take some of the aspects, but not all of the facts, into account. This oversight leads him to the following conclusion: "It was similar inertia if not also the 'business-as-usual' attitude that postponed the uprising in the Warsaw ghetto till hardly any people or any strength was left for fighting, and certainly far too few to make a break-through that might have saved thousands of lives."[60] The uprising was not postponed. It was a matter of common sense that arms had to be manufactured, rifles purchased and smuggled into the ghetto and homemade bombs prepared, before the German Army could be attacked.

The German Jews in Fall of 1938 and the Jews of Warsaw in Spring of 1943 have one thing in common: the "business-as-usual" characteristic. And so have all other European Jews; those who were hiding in Holland or Poland, in Hungary or France.

All the Franks wanted, was to go on with life as much as possible in the usual fashion. This goes for little Anne as well as for the other members of her family. But the Franks did not want to face the facts of survival. They should have had an easy time hiding out singly, each with a different family, because they had excellent connections among gentile Dutch families. "But instead of planning for this, the main principle of their planning was to continue as much as possible with the kind of family life they were accustomed to. Any other course would have meant not merely giving up the beloved family life as usual, but also accepting as reality man's inhumanity to man. Most of all it would have forced their acceptance that business-as-usual was not an absolute value, but sometimes the most destructive of all attitudes. There is little doubt that the Franks, who were able to provide themselves with so much, could have provided themselves with a gun or two had they wished. They could have shot down at least

---

[60]Foreword, Ibidem, p. xi; compare Mishney Evrey Ha-Homah (From the Two Sides of the Wall) by Vlodka-Feigel Peltel Mindzitzki, Kibbutz Ha-Meuhad, Tel Aviv, 1969, which describes the incredible courage in Warsaw.

one or two of the S.S. men who came for them. There was no
surplus of S.S. men . . . They could have sold their lives dearly
instead of walking to their death."[61]

Bettelheim uses oversimplifications in order to prove his point.
It is farfetched to assume even for a moment, that the Franks
could "have had an easy time hiding singly." Even in Holland,
hiding a Jew was very difficult. It was extremely difficult to find
one gentile family with the proper accommodations for a family as
large as the Franks. Severe punishment would result in case the
hidden Jews would be discovered by the Germans. Not too many
Dutchmen were able, ready and willing to risk their lives. Jacob
Presser, whose book is a classic among the books of Holocaust
literature writes: "Local Dutch Nazis with intimate knowledge of
local conditions, would organize 'hunts' and hand hosts and
fugitives alike over to the Germans. Scores of good men fell
victims to these traitors, whose deeds constitute one of the darkest
chapters in the history of the occupation."[62]

Hiding with an Aryan friend was more problematic than
Bettelheim is willing to admit. Joseph L. Lichten writes in the
foreword to Iranek-Osmecki's book: "When the Germans occupied
Warsaw, one of my closest Christian friends agreed to take care of
my daughter. Indeed, he kept her for some time; but he ultimately
sent her back to the ghetto, refusing to take any more of the risks
of caring for a Jewish child. The consequence of his decision was
inevitable—a concentration camp and a gas chamber."[63] Let me
add parenthetically that it took self-sacrificing courage and
stamina to oppose the Germans. Lichten's friend was probably a
decent and honorable man who could not live in constant fear. He
solved the problem by protecting himself.

Not only Jewish refugee families such as the Franks were
hunted, but even Jewish husbands of mixed marriages were subject
to deportation and therefore hounded. The same is true for
half-and-quarter-Jews. Again Presser writes:[64] "Rauter, too, had

---

[61] Foreword, Ibidem, pp. xiii-xiv.

[62] The Destruction of Dutch Jews, Ibidem, p. 382.

[63] He Who Saves One Life, Crown Publishers, New York, p. ix.

[64] The Destruction of Dutch Jews, Ibidem, p. 314.

very little doubt that the Jewish husbands of mixed marriages ought to disappear to Poland . . . In view of all this, it seems almost miraculous that these people, of all, should have been saved; certainly no one would have ventured to predict it at the time . . . They survived, but not without being hounded almost to death. More than once it appeared that their end had come. Not a few of them went into hiding. Did the powerful voice of the Protestant Churches contribute to their survival? Once again the question is difficult to answer." Dutch officials went out of their way to frustrate the Germans' plans regarding these people. But they were not willing to take the risk and to do the same for foreign Jews. The price was too high.

"Securing a gun" is another phrase which Bettelheim repeats quite often. But what good is a gun if the person who has the pistol has not been trained to use it? Securing several guns for all members of the Frank family raises the question: from whom could they have purchased them and where could they have practiced how to use them? Whether the host family, who ran the risk of being taken to a concentration camp, would have permitted the Franks to harbor guns, is another question. Many compassionate gentiles in Holland as well as in other countries were taken to extermination camps, where they perished, because they gave shelter to persecuted Jewish neighbors. "The loss of an S.S. with every Jew arrested" should have been the rule. The Germans arrested Poles, Serbs, Frenchmen and Dutchmen, too, and they could not "sell their lives dearly." It was only when they joined the Underground, where forest and the rivers, the mountains and the fields, and above all, a sympathetic population were their allies, that they could fight selling their lives dearly and imposing casualties upon the Germans.

"Flight to other countries" is another oversimplification. Indeed, some Latin and Central American countries were willing to issue (really sell) visas to Jewish individuals, after they had obtained a certificate of baptism, which again they could buy for money. But no consulate in Europe was willing to do this for Jewish groups or even large families. Some aggressive individuals with money found a way to escape. The masses, poor and helpless, were trapped. There was no possibility of saving themselves. It was possible to apply for a passport and a visa in Germany in Fall, 1938 and even later. But where could a Jew apply for a visa in Poland in Fall of 1939, or in Yugoslavia in Spring of 1941?

Heinrich Liebrecht writes about an experience which was typical of the conditions prevailing in Europe, not only in Germany. "Although I had been a judge myself, I had long ago abandoned all futile attempts to emigrate legally. We had given a Señor Velasco, a doctor connected with the Chilean Consulate, several thousand marks to help us get out of Germany. He was to deliver forged passports and papers and arrange the trip to Switzerland. But though he had promised many times that he would have the papers ready, he always put us off. At last I gave him the choice of delivering the papers or returning the money. I arranged one final meeting. Velasco did not show up. Our last hope was gone and with it most of the money we had set aside for emergencies."[65] Velasco proved to be a close friend of the Gestapo and Liebrecht was sent to Terezin. Velasco was not just a name. It was a symbol. In every country, people like Velasco preyed on Jewish misery. Without Velasco's help, Liebrecht might have survived. He was a convert to Catholicism and served as a volunteer and officer in World War I. Bettelheim's "flight to other countries" theory is fragile, indeed.

Another oversimplified statement which Bettelheim makes is the use of "forged papers." While it is true that sometimes "forged papers" helped Jews to survive for a while, it is also true that the Germans very quickly discovered how to check them. Their helpers were "Kapos" of all national and ethnic groups, who assisted them wholeheartedly. If the Gestapo officers were unable to discover the falsified papers or documents, then their helpers did it for them.

Bettelheim criticizes the European Jews, who did not emigrate "when the time and the means were available." This means for Austrian Jews before March 13, 1938, for Czechoslovakian Jewry before March 15, 1939, and for the Jewish Community in Poland before September 1, 1939. The sequence of these events happened within one and one-half years. By this time millions of Jews were trapped at the mercy of the German Reich. The only countries which had the means, organization and power to act were the Anglo-Saxons. But they lacked the understanding and willingness to do so.

---

[65] We Survived, edited by Eric M. Boehm, New Haven, Yale University Press, 1949, p. 214

The initiative to be really helpful and to rescue lives was lost in the labyrinth of politics and intrigues. The policy of Roosevelt's administration was complicated by duplicity. There were two camps in his administration: those who insisted that the refugee presented a threat to national security, and those who insisted that humanitarian roots of the New Deal should be applied. The President appeared at home in either camp. "Neither side knew for certain where Roosevelt would stand at a given moment. This absence of a specific mandate, which some observers see as the most typical of Roosevelt's style of administration, was very apparent on the rescue question."[66] We know this today to be a fact: when issues have to be solved, where life and death hang in the balance, this kind of politics would hamper the humanitarian mission of America.

Bettelheim concludes the foreword with a philosophical observation: "Those who seek to protect the body at all costs die many times over. Those who risk the body to survive as men have a good chance to live on."[67] He regards the Frank family as the embodiment of the blindness which afflicted Europe's Jews. The Franks, who symbolize the tragedy of European Jewry, do not represent the European Jewish Community-at-large. Eastern European Jews consisted of workers, artisans, farmers, small shopkeepers, as well as professionals and business merchants. Thousands of Jewish youth in Poland for instance went through obligatory military training. The Jewish working masses and militant Zionist groups were totally different from the West European, such as the middle class Franks. This fact does not denigrate the Franks but rather points out the irrelevance of Bettelheim's oversimplifications and the misleading conclusions of his thesis. These masses were exterminated everywhere because they were minorities caught between two hostile majorities. They were not given a chance to fight.

As we look at other nations under Hitler's terror we see a similar situation everywhere. Ten thousand Russian prisoners-of-war were shot in full view of the terrified civilian population. They

---

[66] Henry Feingold, "The Politics of Rescue," Rutgers University Press, New Brunswick, New Jersey, p. xii.

[67] Foreword, Ibidem, p. xviii.

did not revolt. Polish intellectuals and army officers were murdered by the Germans. They, too, died without resistance. Nor did the inhabitants of Lidice revolt when they were massacred. Neither did the villagers in the Ukraine and White Russia revolt. The French did not rebel when they were abducted in the "Nacht und Nebel" action. There was no resistance on the part of more than one hundred thousand Poles in Lublin when their children, suitable for "Germanization," were taken from the parents. Why did not the Serbs revolt when whole villages were annihilated?

It seems that revolts do not occur casually, by chance. They are governed by rigid laws: political, strategic, social and psychological. Such laws are applicable to all peoples and nations throughout the world. The partisan movement along the Eastern front appeared as a reality only after the defeat of the Germans at Stalingrad. A revolt does not break out spontaneously. Conditions must be met before it actually begins. The Warsaw revolt did not break out until the summer of 1944, five years after the collapse of Poland.[68]

The European Jews were in an exceptionally peculiar and vulnerable position, which paralysed every possibility of resistance and self-defense. During Hitler's domination the peoples of Europe were divided into categories. The difference between the Ukraine and Holland, Lithuania and Italy, Slovakia and Bulgaria, France and Poland, Denmark and Hungary, explains why it was much more difficult to save a Jew in Lwow, Kovno, Riga, Bralislava, Warsaw and Budapest than it was in Amsterdam, Rome, Sofia, Brussels, Paris and Copenhagen. The Lithuanians, Latvians, Ukrainians, Croats, Hungarians and the Poles, made the Jewish minority helpless, vulnerable and defenseless.

Under these circumstances the Jews could not have done any more that would have basically changed their fate. Nations and countries were unprepared to face the menace, and even more so were their Jewish citizens. Heroism, resistance and strategy, in an organized fashion, could have produced results, if they would have been led from the outside, "from forces more powerful than they themselves could have mustered. But a mass of six million Jews could not have escaped to the forests, or have hidden among

[68] K. Shabbetai, As Sheep to the Slaughter, New York-Tel Aviv, 1963.

Gentiles, or have obtained arms . . . Caught in the trap of Nazi
horrors, there was no escape, no rescue."[69] All roads led to doom.
Their deliverance could have come from the outside only. But the
outside world erected a high wall of indifference, hatred and
selfishness. Hindsight wisdom and advice, reckless generalizations
and rationalization, oversimplifications wrapped in scholarly terminology, will not change the realities of the Holocaust era one
iota.

Dr. Hannah Arendt is a well-known political scientist. She
earned a worldwide reputaion with her learned, socio-political
books and articles. Her writings are both scholarly and controversial. Arendt's attitude and interpretation of the Holocaust,
criticism of European Jews at large and the conclusion which she
has reached, are not isolated. She represents, together with
historians R. Hilberg, G. Reitlinger, H.R. Trevor-Roper and
psychiatrist B. Bettelheim, a school of thought which merits our
full attention. These scholars have another characteristic in
common as a group, namely, complete ignorance of the extremely
extensive material about the period of the Holocaust published in
Hebrew and Yiddish. Furthermore they all praise the Israelis for
their fighting spirit and heroism. They criticize the European Jews
for their passive obedience and submissiveness.

Norman Podhoretz, editor of the Commentary, described
Arendt's book "Eichmann in Jerusalem: A Report on the
Banality of Evil,"[70] as "A Study in the Perversity in Bril-
liance."[71] A student of totalitarianism, she employs the technique
of improper generalization, which enables her to reach one-sided
conclusions. When her five articles appeared in The New Yorker in
February and March, 1963, as a report on the Eichmann trial in
Jerusalem, the voices of disagreement rose very high. The
resentment came from all corners of the globe, after notable men
and women presented their points of view. Among them were
Jacob Robinson, Marie Syrkin, Ernst Simon, Alexander Donat,
Norman Podhoretz, Lionel Abel and a score of others.

Arendt deals with Jewish communal organizations, Jewish party
and welfare associations, on both the local and international level.

[69] Alexander Donat, Judaism, Fall, 1963, p. 432.

[70] New York, Viking Press, 1963.

[71] Commentary, September, 1963, pp. 201-8.

Her conclusion is: "Wherever Jews lived, there were recognized Jewish leaders, and these leaders, almost without exception, cooperated in one way or another, for one reason or another, with the Nazis. The whole truth was that if the Jewish people had really been unorganized and leaderless there would have been chaos and plenty of misery but the total number of victims would hardly have been between five and six million."[72]

The Jews had no land, no government, no arms. They represented thousands of large and small communities which were separated from each other by fjords, mountains, rivers and seas, as well as by socio-political and religio-cultural frontiers. National or international cooperation of Jewish communities, under the Nazis, in occupied territories, did not exist. The Nazis saw to it that there should be no communication or exchange of ideas among those who were doomed to extermination. The moment the Stukas dropped their last bombs, the country or region was hermetically sealed off from its neighbors.

Arendt's appraisal of a very difficult and complex situation produced a highly exaggerated picture of what the Jewish communities could have done and accomplished were they led by courageous leaders. The Yugoslav partisans led by Josip Broz Tito had an army and arms. Above all they were at home, whether in the mountains or in the forests. In spite of this, two million Yugoslavs out of a population of eighteen million lost their lives. The Yugoslavs faced the enemy under different circumstances for four, not six years.

The German army experienced difficulties after the winter of 1941-2. It concentrated its efforts on the East front, giving the Yugoslav partisan a chance to prepare for action.

The German Army was well-organized and equipped. Those who planned World War II undermined to the fullest, from the inside, each country they attacked. The "use" of local fascists and followers, to whom they promised independence, was planned in advance. They also utilized the local Volksbund. There were times when the Jews must have felt that all of Europe, from the Atlantic to the Black Sea, "collaborated" with the Germans. When Laval declared: "I believe in and wish Germany's victory" he added to the existing cooperation with the German authorities which was

[72] Marie Syrkin, Jewish Frontier, May, 1963, pp. 7-14.

universal throughout occupied Europe. "Every village official from Norway to Sicily, from Holland to Greece, was confronted by a similar decision. Wisely or foolishly, bravely or cravenly, they had to choose between order and no order, and the only order to be chosen was the Nazi order."[73] The resistance movements in occupied Europe came too late to be of any effective assistance to the decimated and fragmented Jewish population.

According to Arendt, the Nazis needed, above all, Jewish cooperation in order to implement the "Final Solution" against the European Jews. She thinks they received it to the fullest. But she also admits "the totality of the moral collapse the Nazis caused in respectable European society—not only in Germany but in almost all countries." A demoralized European society unable to live up to the crucial test in time of crisis, the hostile attitude of the local populace towards their Jewish neighbors, made escape unsuitable and defense impossible. Even where the local populace was sympathetic, survival was highly problematic.

Let me give an illustration: In September, 1940, a group of daring Jews in Austria—men, women and children—bought a freighter and crossed the Danube to Yugoslavia. Their destination, of course, was Palestine. However, they were not permitted to continue the journey, because Yugoslavia's neighbors, as well as the British, would not issue visas. They were forced to live on the freighter for months. Later they were recognized as refugees and found asylum in the town of Shabats (Shabac) in Serbia. Two hundred of them—mostly children—left Shabats in 1940-41. In April, 1941 the Germans occupied Yugoslavia and found 1100 refugees and 100 local Jews in the town. On September 24, 1941, all 5,000 male Serbs, age 14-70 and all Jews in Shabats were arrested and ordered to "race" 50 miles (after having been kept for two nights and one day without food) and then brought back to the town. Subsequently, the Jews were "annihilated." Only two women of the 1200 Jews survived the war. This is how Jewish refugees lived and fought for survival.

The obstacles to survival were overwhelming. When the Germans entered a city, the "Volksbund" was waiting for them with a complete list of the leaders of the Jewish community who would be found and arrested in a few hours.

[73] Oscar Handlin, Commentary, November, 1962, p. 404.

The psychological impact of the Danube episode upon Jews in Austria, who might have been encouraged by the success of the freighter's landing in Palestine, was devastating. Jewish refugees from Poland, Danzig and Czechoslovakia, who were trapped in Austria, could not encourage their relatives and friends to follow in the footsteps of those on the freighter. The destiny of the refugees hung in the air for months. The International Red Cross knew about the freighter, its passengers and the miserable conditions. The Allies, primarily British, did everything possible to prevent other freighters from entering the Danube by putting pressure on Yugoslavia and Rumania to watch over the entrance into the Blue River. The heroic struggle of daring men and women ended in tragedy, because the Allies did not permit them to survive. Their disaster was planned and executed by the Germans. The actions of the Allies were sinister and underhanded. Both the executioners and the bystanders were morally responsible jointly for the tragic end of the victims. The innocent Serbs paid dearly for their sympathetic help and understanding of the homeless and the hunted.

Any generalization concerning the Holocaust can be challenged.[74] The Judenraete (The Jewish Councils) differed from country to country. Any generalized judgment condemning the Jewish Councils is unfair. As far as the Jewish Councils are concerned, Belgium and France differed from Bulgaria and Italy, as did Hungary from Rumania and Slovakia from Croatia. To speak generally of Jewish leaders in Europe during the Holocaust, and to single out special cases, which are indeed vulnerable, means to indulge in oversimplifications for the sake of distorting the whole picture. What Hannah Arendt demands of the victims of mass extermination, and especially of their representatives and leaders, is a leadership which would have made them sages, saints and heroes, all at the same time. No nation on this or the other side of the Atlantic, or for that matter in the world, came even close to it.

There were no Judenraete in occupied Soviet Union, because there were no centrally organized Jewish communities and there was no central Jewish leadership. Nevertheless the extermination

---

[74] Ernst Simon, Judaism, Fall, 1963, p. 393.

of Jews in the U.S.S.R. was as complete—without the Juden-raete—as in the other parts of Central and Western Europe.

In order to understand Arendt's accusation that "locally recognized Jewish leaders" became members of Jewish Councils one must remember that the Judenraete were organized by the Germans long before crematoria were in sight. In other words, they came into being long before the implementation of the "Final Solution." Furthermore, as a rule, members of Judenraete were mostly obscure individuals, appointed by the Nazis. "In smaller communities the Nazis usually appointed the entire mem-bership of the Judenraete; in the big cities they merely appointed the Chairman and imposed upon him the task of providing twelve or twenty-four associates."[75] To live in a ghetto, or in a restricted area in the West, meant to provide the necessities of survival for the next hour ("hayey shaa"). No one has ever suggested that this was not an important function.

The governments of the occupied countries felt no need to apologize for mayors in cities and towns, and administrators in villages, who accepted such responsibilities under the Nazis. If life were to continue, difficult as it was, then someone had to be responsible and do the day to day job; to provide food and clothing, to bring comfort to the sick and aged, to bury the dead. Someone had to see that water and electricity were available, as well as a score of other necessities. Mutatis mutandur, the members of the Judenraete acted similarly, although their only hope and prayer were Hitler's defeat. "Their strategy and political judgment, were part of a desperate—and, alas, a losing—effort to buy time, to alleviate suffering, to save lives. The Jewish leaders in the ghettos ran the full gamut of types—from saints and martyrs, to pragmatic and cunning 'catastrophe statesmen' and survival strategists, to a small minority (whose numbers increased with the deepening disaster) of opportunists, adverturers, weaklings, dupes, and power-hungry fanatics. But there were no collaborators among them, no Quislings, who served the enemy ideologically and politically."[76]

The Jewish situation was more abnormal than the Gentile. There was every moral justification, at least at the beginning of

---

[75] Alexander Donat, Judaism, Fall, 1963, p. 417.

[76] Alexander Donat, Ibidem, p. 425.

World War II, to assist and help the Jews, wherever they might have been living. That some decent men were trapped, some weak men became brutalized and demoralized, does not suggest that the idea of serving in time of great crisis should be degraded. Above all it does not mean that the idea of serving one's fellow Jews should be debased. It is very difficult for an outsider to understand how normal human beings can become involved in abnormal situations. The psychological difficulty to comprehend it is far greater! How can anyone want to live, plan, or exist, not knowing whether he will live through the "next hour"? "Hayey shaa" living is abnormal, therefore extremely difficult. It was possible to serve others on the basis of "one hour" of existence because duty-bound men did not think of the next hour. Live today, this hour. Fulfill your duty now, and meet the challenge of the next day, the next hour, as it arrives.

Generalizations must lead necessarily to distortions. Hannah Arendt tells us that Adolf Eichmann and his horde turned to "the Zionists as a matter of course." The Nazis decided to negotiate in the summer of 1944. They asked as a ransom for a million Jews, ten thousand trucks, among other things, to be used on the Eastern Front. During the last few months of the War, Joel Brand's name appeared in the Anglo-Saxon press as the spokesman for the remnant of European Jewry.[77] Dr. Arendt claims that "the Zionists were free to come practically as they pleased; they were exempt from wearing the yellow star; they received permits to visit concentration camps in Hungary. . . . "[78] It is a matter of fact that from March 17, 1944 until October 15, 1944 the Jews in Hungary were under the "protection" of three rulers, at one and the same time. Sztójay, and later on General Lakatos, presided over the official governments, while the Szálasi Nyilas (Arrow and Cross) Party governed unofficially. The Gestapo, cleverly supervised by A. Eichmann and his deputies Krumey, Wisliceny and Becher, reigned unofficially and discreetly. No one sound of mind in Spring 1944 trusted a Nazi permit. By that time too many people, particularly Jews, knew the Nazi secret. This is not contradicted by the fact that Joel Brand travelled via Vienna to Istanbul and Rezsö Kastner kept company with Kurt Becher.

[77] Alex Weissberg, Desperate Mission, Criterion Books, New York, 1958.

[78] Jewish Frontier, Ibidem, p. 9.

While the "bargaining" was going on hundreds of members of the Hashomer Hatzair youth movement were arrested and lost their lives.[79] The gentle leader of the Zionist movement in Hungary, engineer Otto Komoly was among the murdered. Nyilas terror reigned in Pest from middle October until the end of December, 1944 and in Buda until the middle of February, 1945. From October 15 on, their terror was accompanied by chaos and Red Army bombing. Jewish victims were murdered in cold blood at night time. Their bodies were thrown into the Danube. These martyrs numbered into the thousands. Zionists were no exception. However young Zionists organized resistance bunkers and were often betrayed by their neighbors.

Joel Brand was a humble and modest man. Although unassuming he rose to prominence not because he wanted to be prominent but rather because no one cared to do what he was willing to undertake. The Brands were willing to open their doors to Jews from Slovakia, Poland and Yugoslavia who crossed illegally into Hungary and had to be housed on the spur of the moment. The Rescue Committee would then provide them with papers, housing and financial help. Among the German Gestapo couriers and agents traveling to and from Istanbul were men who were willing to take letters to and bring answers from members of the Jewish Agency in Turkey. Brand, a simple, good-hearted and courageous man, was the liaison between the Rescue Committee in Budapest and the Zionists in Istanbul.

When A. Eichmann began to "officiate" in Budapest after March 17, 1944, Brand, known in Gestapo circles, became his choice as representative of the Jews. Ultimately Eichmann asked Brand to fly to Turkey. His order was "accepted," not because the Jews or Zionists in Hungary had any confidence in him but because the situation was desperate and stalling for precious time was the only possible solution. That was the time when Zionists were granted special privileges of meeting with Eichmann's henchmen without wearing the yellow star. After all, the Hungarians knew that something was going on, and would have been even more suspicious seeing Jews wearing a yellow star visiting S.S. headquarters or being seen in their company. The two legitimate leaders of the Jewish Communities in Budapest,

[79] Hashomer Hatzair—Borochow Kör, Budapest, 1948.

Councilor Samu Stern (neolog) and Philipp von Freudiger (orthodox) were glad to relinquish this kind of responsibility to Joel Brand and his colleagues, younger men who were daring, courageous and aggressive. To label this as Zionism in action is ridiculous.

Richard H.S. Crossman, a man of great distinction, was naive to write, as late as summer, 1958, that "it was surely unfair to suggest that Roosevelt and Churchill were callous about the Jews as Weissberg-Brand stated."[80] The fact remains that the leaders of the Allies did not show any enthusiasm for rescuing Jews whether they were in Budapest, Bucharest or any other European capital. Diligent and meticulous research was done by YIVO followed by Yad Vashem. Lately the Hebrew University, Brandeis University and other institutes in many parts of the World have joined in the research. They were instrumental in a trend that will ultimately lead to a complete re-evaluation of the meaning of the Holocaust. So far four stages are clearly noticeable.

1. The victims were guilty; because of their passivity, cowardice, obedience, submissiveness and complete collaboration and even identification with the perpetrators of the crime. These characteristics of the victims were the result of a long "galut" (diaspora) history of oppression, persecution and hostility based on religio-social prejudice. It culminated in the act of planned annihilation.

2. The second stage spoke of the determination of the murderers and the hopeless predicament of the victims. The "Final Solution" was conceived by a satanic determination to murder, destroy, exterminate and wipe out. The "solution" had to be "final." It was possible for the murderers to "strike the blow" because the victims were isolated and unorganized in their efforts to resist.

3. Books related to the third stage speak of the victims having been trapped between highly-organized and technologically-superior murderers and their corrupted, demoralized helpers. The helpers numbered millions (Latvians, Lithuanians, Poles, Ukrainians, Hungarians, Croatians, Slovakians, Rumanians and even Dutch, Flemish, Norwegian and French ascarids).

[80]Midstream summer, 1958, pp. 95-7 and autumn, 1958, pp. 99-100.

4. Publications of the fourth stage explain why the Six Million victims, residing as groups all over Europe and separated from each other, could not fight back energetically and resist more effectively. Their brothers, friends and neighbors remained silent. History teaches that heroism has its own laws and cannot blossom in a desert of callousness and indifference.

In a sense the group led by Hilberg, Reitlinger, Trevor-Roper, Bettelheim and Arendt deserve our thanks. They helped to accelerate the research and to publish details, which even the finest memory can not retain forever.

The Religio-Theological Aspect

We Jews are a God-oriented people. The ability of Jewish genius to interpret varied phenomena of each age, dark or enlightened, bears witness to its creative power. Very seldom have we neglected to debate the meaning of disturbing, extraordinary occurrences of history. We were able to seek out answers as to why these events occurred, what they meant to us and to the rest of the world.

We have been unable, so far, to create a religio-theological interpretation of the phenomenon and meaning of the Holocaust for ourselves and for our modern age! This challenging fact remains unanswered although our generation needs, desperately, an honest answer, instead of apologies. The search for the purpose of Jewish existence and its meaning to the Jewish people are closely linked to the Holocaust and our age. There is today a renascent pride and an awakening of Jewish identity. Both demand answers to the questions "What happened" and "For whose sake were we slaughtered every day. . . ?" The human voice in the Jew is tempted to go one step further and to ask: If I was created in the image of God, was the Nazi who slew my mother created in the image of the same God?

We shall see, in the following pages, how the Jewish thinkers [81] have tried to answer "the question of all questions." Among them

---

[81] Seymour Cain writes: "Christian theologians have neglected to deal with Auschwitz. Many Christian theologians, especially those of the Auschwitz generation, have been deeply affected in their hearts and minds . . . by the event. I am simply saying that it is not dwelt on (usually not even mentioned) in their considered, explicit theological works, even when they deal with such themes as God's action in history or the historicity of God." Judaism, Summer 1971, p. 283.

are: Leo Baeck, Martin Buber, and to make the distinction between the living and the dead, Mordecai M. Kaplan, Abraham J. Heschel, Jacob B. Agus, Ignaz Maybaum, Richard L. Rubenstein and Arthur A. Cohen.

Leo Baeck was one of the few indispensable greats, who was chosen to lead his people in time of extreme crisis. Terezin (Theresienstadt) was not a concentration camp in the usual sense. He was taken there on January 27, 1943. Baeck and Green report that there were even visits and inspections in 1944 to the Paradeis-ghetto by the International Red Cross and the Danish Red Cross. During the visit Judenaeltester (eldest of the Jewish Council) Epstein wore a pressed black suit. He was chauffered around by an S.S. man, who opened the door of Epstein's car and bowed.[82] The effect on the morale of the interned was devastating. They felt forgotten and forsaken. Nevertheless Baeck knew of the existence of busses with gassing mechanism since 1941, while still in Berlin. He was informed about crematoria at Terezin by a competent man, engineer Gruenberg, half Jew, who came back from Auschwitz. However he decided to be silent. Baeck did not discuss the existence of the chimneys with the leaders of the Judenrat in Terezin. A saint does not make suffering and dying for others more difficult. He felt that the inmates would not benefit from this information. "Living in the expectation of death by gassing would only be the harder. So I came to the grave decision to tell no one."[83]

Among Baeck's books and treatises written and published after 1945 there is hardly any reference to the greatest of all tragedies in Jewish history. I found one brief paragraph about the Nazi terror which reads: "Peace was profaned; and a profaned peace brings an even worse destiny than a breach of peace. War always follows it, a worse war than that caused by a broken peace."[84]

Leo Baeck was, without any doubt, a man of God. He was a shining star in the darkness of a very long night, and a pillar of strength in time of calamity and despair. The saintly scholar

---

[82] Gerald Green, The Artist of Terezin, Hawthorn Books, Inc., Publishers, New York, 1969, pp. 88-90.

[83] We Survived, New Haven, Yale University Press, pp. 285-298.

[84] This Peoples Israel: The Meaning of Jewish Existence, The Jewish Publication Society, 1965, pp. 385-6.

lectured in Terezin, comforted the old and sick, encouraged the meek and disillusioned. Baeck represented God's people before and after Terezin. It is indeed surprising that he preferred not to discuss in his post-war writings any of the aspects of the Holocaust, including the religio-theological meaning of it.

It is not easy to accept this as a matter of fact, or to understand, under the circumstances, why he did not feel the need to deal with the problem. Historians often raise questions, a posteriori, because they were not answered in due time. The greatness of Leo Baeck, the Rabbi, Scholar and Philosopher, will not be diminished by pondering over his unique role, greatness and the vacuum which he left in his legacy, by not discussing the Holocaust.

Twentieth-century man is living in one of the world's most challenging periods, unprecedented in history. He has the moral responsibility to explain good and evil, and why modern man reacts to them as he does. If the guidance of great minds, the wisdom of sages and the experience of saints can be most helpful in time of crisis, then the name of Leo Baeck is unfortunately missing from the list among the thinkers who wrote about the catastrophe.

This is not simply a matter of curiosity which bothers us. What makes us discontent is the fact of being unable to benefit from his wisdom and experience. Regretably Baeck did not share with us his first hand knowledge of the Holocaust. His close friend, the late Michael Guttman, read to me in Budapest of 1942 a letter which Baeck was able to mail to him from Berlin. He wrote in his letter about the closing of the academy for the Study of Judaism which was so dear to him. To the living, Leo Baeck remains a classic and heroic case of human survival which triumphed over destruction. He shared the faith of his ancestors as deeply and passionately after Terezin as he did before, and the reflection on the existence of the Jewish people filled him with wonder and enthusiasm.

In comparison with Leo Baeck, whose visits to Germany after World War II were Jewishly motivated, another sage and saint of our time, Martin Buber, visited Germany officially several times after 1945. He did so for the purpose of addressing the German people and institutions. On such occasions Buber spoke about his relationship to the German people and culture. It was inevitable to be silent and he spoke about Hitlerism and the Holocaust. Buber received the Hanseatic Goethe Prize, given to him by the University of Hamburg in 1952, and the Peace Prize of the German Book Trade in 1953.

We find Buber's speech in the volume, A Believing Humanism, delivered on the occasion of his visit when he received the Peace Prize.[85] He stated his position as follows: "About a decade ago a considerable number of Germans—there must have been many thousands of them—under the indirect command of the German Government and the direct command of its representatives, killed millions of my people in a systematically prepared and executed procedure whose organized cruelty cannot be compared with any previous historical event. I, who am one of those who remained alive, have only in a formal sense a common humanity with those who took part in this action. They have so radically removed themselves from the human sphere, so transposed themselves into a sphere of monstrous inhumanity inaccessible to my conception, that not even hatred, much less an overcoming of hatred, was able to arise in me. And what am I that I could here presume to 'forgive'!"

When Theodor Heuss, President of the German Republic, stepped down, Buber greeted him as the writer of history and the scholar of statehood. Buber wrote: "And here in the Land your name is named, then one means by that above all the man 'who came after Hitler.' This does not signify, of course, the notion that in place of Hitler Germany, that meant for us the martyr's death of millions of our people, you had established an 'other' Germany. Something of the sort does not take place even in the easiest of cases, and that was certainly the most difficult of its kind in world history. . . ."[86]

On these occasions Buber would speak about the Holocaust as a Jew. However there are no references that he explored the religio-philosophical aspect of it in his post-War writings.

Buber formulated "The Question" as follows: "From the moment when a national disaster appears inevitable, and especially after it has become a reality, it can, like every great torment,

---

[85] Simon and Schuster, A publication of Credo Perspectives, New York, 1969, pp. 195-202.

[86] Ibidem, pp. 215-6.

become a productive force from the religious point of view: it begins to suggest new questions and to stress old ones. Dogmatized conceptions are pondered afresh in the light of the events, and the faith relationship that has to stand the test of an utterly changed situation is renewed in a modified form. But the new acting force is nothing less than the force of extreme despair, a despair so elemental that it can have one of two results; the sapping of the last will of life, or the renewal of the soul."[87]

In the treatise, Eclipse of God, Buber wrote: "Twice in the history of mankind—insofar as it can be surveyed and understood by man—there has been an attempt to bind the radical distinction between good and evil to the Absolute. The two manifestations of this great enterprise of the spirit are, to be sure, as different as possible in their nature and course of development." Then he continued: "The first manifestation appeared in Oriental and Greek antiquity. The crisis of the second great attempt to bind the ethical to the Absolute extends into our time. It finds its actual beginning in Feuerbach's critique of religion.[88] With Nietzsche the values of good—evil were replaced by the values of strong—weak. He proclaimed a biologically-based morality. 'I teach negation of all that weakens, I teach affirmation of all that strengthens.' "

While Buber speaks of the eclipse of God he seems to be more interested in repudiating Jungian Psychology than to focus on good and evil and bringing it in relationship to our age. From C.G. Jung, who lived in and served Germany during World War II, to the Holocaust, is one small step. Buber never has made this step. In Anthologies of Jewish thinking in the aftermath of the Holocaust the saintly name of Buber is painfully and conspicuously absent.

Reconstructionism has made a tremendous contribution to Jewish life both in the Diaspora and in Israel. It has taken a firm stand on vital issues concerning Jewish civilization (religion, culture, ethics, arts, social justice). It underlines the centrality of Jewish peoplehood; how we survived in the past, what is our present status and what our plans for the future should be. Evaluating numerous books and essays written by Mordecai M. Kaplan, the greatest living sage of our time and founder of

[87] The Prophetic Faith, Harper and Brothers, New York, 1960, p. 183.

[88] Harper and Brothers Publishers, New York, 1957, p. 99, p. 108-111.

Reconstructionism, one finds very little that he wrote about the Holocaust and its meaning.

Kaplan's attitude towards theodicies will partly justify and explain why he might have been reluctant to deal with a subject "which has no satisfactory answer to offer." It is an age-old question, "why God, who is both omniscient and omnipotent does not use his omniscience and omnipotence to forestall the evil that man does?[89]

"In the past, theologians wrote lengthy poetical or philosophical theodicies in which they tried to justify the ways of God to man. When, however, we not only reify, or hypostatize, but also absolutize, Godhood, we are confronted by a logical dilemma. That is to say, if we assume that God is absolutely omnipotent, we cannot possibly allow for the existence of anything that might even attempt to resist or oppose Him. On the other hand, if we do not wish to delude ourselves, we cannot deny the existence of evil which, by its very nature, is the antithesis of Godhood. Not a single one of the numerous theodicies, or attempts of thinkers to reconcile the goodness of God with the existence of evil, has ever proved convincing.

"We might, perhaps, resolve the dilemma by assuming that God's omnipotence is not an actually realized fact at any point of time, but a potenial fact. That is to say, if we take into account the infinite duration of Godhood, it is possible to conceive that the evil which now mars the cosmos will ultimately be eliminated. Or we might become resigned to the intrinsic inability of the human mind to resolve the dilemma, except by the practical effort to reduce the amount of evil in the world, so as to leave the world the better for our having lived in it.

"The atrocities perpetrated against six million Jewish victims by the Nazis, and the similar suffering imposed on many other human beings by Nazi, Fascist, and Communist persecution, and by the armies of both sides in recent wars, constitute a tragedy of such dimensions that no posthumous reward can compensate for it, or explain it away. Nor can we blame human sinfulness for the misery caused by earthquakes, floods, pestilences, and other natural catastrophes.

[89]M. M. Kaplan, Questions Jews Ask, Reconstructionist Press, New York, 1956, pp. 115-124.

"Tradition, therefore, offers no solution to the problem of evil, which can satisfy the spirit of our generation. It is not surprising that Samson Raphael Hirsch, the founder of the Neo-Orthodox movement, has no satisfactory answer to offer to this question. But neither have such non-Orthodox Jewish theologians as Solomon Schechter and Kaufmann Kohler, or, among living Jewish thinkers, Leo Baeck and Martin Buber. Yet this question is at the very heart of the religious crisis of our day. We are sorely in need of a conception of God which is compatible with a satisfactory orientation to the problem of evil.

"It is, therefore, most regrettable that the institutions which train spiritual leaders are apparently afraid to grapple with this problem. I have long been wrestling with the problem myself and have arrived at a solution which is satisfactory to me."

Kaplan taught in the 1950s when "Questions" were published at the Jewish Theological Seminary of New York. He might have been confronted with questions related to evil generally and to the Holocaust particularly, as well as the widespread pessimism with regard to human nature. Kaplan addresses himself to the mood of pessimism prevalent in our modern society.

"Pessimism is more the reflection of a mood than a legitimate conclusion based on an analysis of the facts. Fearful thinking is at least as dangerous and misleading as wishful thinking.

"Another factor in producing the mood that is responsible for this pessimism is the growing awareness of the compulsive drives which prevent the individual from achieving an integrated well-balanced personality, and society from achieving peace and cooperation among men. Finally, pessimism is supported by the tendency of the troubled mind to seek an escape from the harsh realities of the present in the contemplation of a romanticized version of the past.

"But if we submit the actual facts about human life, past and present, to objective analysis, we see that the pessimism born of the anxieties of our age is not warranted. Hitler's mass slaughter of Jews and other victims was, indeed, of unprecedented scope and extent, but qualitatively, it was not different from the massacres perpetrated by the Crusading hordes against Jews and Saracens in the Middle Ages, or from other massacres in earlier times.

"To be sure, there is plenty of evil in the world today, some of it not anticipated in past eras. In some respects, we may even have deteriorated under the impact of new problems which are as yet unsolved. But there are also great manifestations of good.

"We must insist on and persist in the faith that all evils which we can identify as such, we can, by the application of the mental and spiritual powers with which God has endowed us, eventually overcome. If we cannot believe in the potentialities of human nature, we have nothing on which to base our faith in the goodness of God."

However it was surprising that Kaplan remained silent when Richard L. Rubenstein published After Auschwitz, and actually challenged all Jewish religious philosophies including Reconstructionism. Rubenstein's outcry that "God is dead" and his pessimism about our civilization, based on Freud's predicament about human potentialities, was a challenge in particular to Reconstructionism. It is our firm belief that meaningful comfort, solace and understanding could and should have come from its headquarters. A Modern Functional Rationale must include the Holocaust. If "the purpose of Jewish existence is to be a People in the image of God," and if "the meaning of Jewish existence is to foster in ourselves as Jews ... a sense of moral responsibility in action,"[90] then our existence and action would be fortified by understanding the correlation between these two principles and the Holocaust. Grateful generations of Rabbis and laymen alike would appreciate hearing from their master and teacher.

Our generation has written a "new Book of Job" in search of an answer and the vindication of God, in view of the existence of evil. Abraham J. Heschel has given us a new conception of the Hiding God. "For us, contemporaries and survivors of history's most terrible horrors, it is impossible to meditate about the compassion of God without asking: Where is God?[91]

"The mark of Cain on the face of man has come to overshadow the likeness of God. There has never been so much distress, agony and terror. It is often sinful for the sun to shine. At no time has the earth been so soaked with blood. Fellow-men have turned out to be evil spirits, monstrous and weird." God was expelled, God is in exile. He is hiding, waiting for men to look for him.

[90] M. M. Kaplan, The Purpose and Meaning of Jewish Existence, Philadelphia, 1964, p. 318.

[91] Man is not Alone, The Jewish Publication Society of America, 1951, pp. 151-176.

In discussing this aspect of the Holocaust one encounters difficulties. Whenever institutional and personal loyalties enter into the picture they ought not to obscure independent research, and above all the truth. Greatness is relative, but truth is absolute. Our sages in the past have glanced over the painful reaction of our generation to the Holocaust. The importance of understanding the greatest of all tragedies for the survival of the Jewish people is eminent. It is indeed very difficult to understand how leading teachers can be silent while their disciples are waiting for their masters to speak.

Our sages included—after a lengthy discussion—the Book of Esther into the "canon" of the Holy Scriptures. God's name is not mentioned, even once, in the ten chapters of the scroll of Esther. But the sword of annihilation, hanging over the Persian Jewry, and the victorious survival made the episode a significant aspect of Jewish History. The sages felt that it was mandatory to include Esther in the Hebrew Bible. Later on, Purim was introduced to remember the danger of annihilation and the miraculous survival. American seminaries have left, regretably, research into and writing of Holocaust history to secular institutions: YIVO, (INSTITUTE FOR JEWISH RESEARCH), YAD VASHEM, Brandeis University and lately Hebrew University. These institutions have been leading in research and in publishing hundreds of volumes, covering every conceivable aspect of the Holocaust.

Evil existed before Auschwitz, and is still in existence after World War II. Religious philosophers must lead in the discussion of evil—including the Holocaust—even if the philosophic inquiry should leave some of the questions unanswered. Not to deal with the Holocaust at all means to leave the modern Jew, who has become increasingly uncomfortable with his modernity, in a vacuum. The research into the religio-philosophical aspect of the Holocaust must be done in places where Jewish religion is being primarily taught, analyzed and expanded. Silence on the subject is unacceptable.

In view of the diversity of trends within the stream of Jewish thought one must appreciate the increasing religio-philosophical interest in the tragic fate of the Six Million. Addresses, papers, sermons and even a small body of books have been presented by Jacob B. Agus, Ignaz Maybaum, Richard L. Rubenstein and Emil

L. Fackenheim.[92] They represent various theological and philosophical schools and attempts in dealing with the problem of the Holocaust and contemporary evil. They all have one thing in common: the determination to search for an answer. For as they discuss, debate and declaim the overwhelming, catastrophic dimensions of the Holocaust they achieve a common denominator. Their outcry is more meaningful than a timid and benumbed silence. Heschel put it very well (quoting Numbers Rabba 15, 16) when he wrote: "At the end of the days, evil will be conquered by the one; in historic times, evil must be conquered one by one." [93] As long as evil exists among us questions must be raised. We must search for answers. Naturally, the response can not be univocal. It will vary from thinker to thinker. The thinker's mode of envisioning God, history and the human situation will determine his answer to a great degree.[94]

Arthur A. Cohen's book, Arguments and Doctrines,[95] represents an impressive array of essays on various theological, philosophical and literary issues. Most of them were written after World War II, but only very few of them deal directly with the Holocaust. Cohen calls his anthology "a reader of Jewish thinking in the aftermath of the Holocaust." To be sure the writers have been influenced by the catastrophe, but their essays don't contribute too much to the understanding of it. Ernst Simon's essay, "Are We Israelis Still Jews?" or Irving Kristol's article "God and the Psychoanalysts" is not helping us at all to understand Teutonism, the ramifications of the "Final Solution" and the homo germanus.

Moses Maimonides wrote his Guide for the Perplexed in the twelfth century. The Guide made its way with amazing rapidity. It received enthusiastic reception upon its publication. The Guide was a success because it dealt with and answered those questions

---

[92] God and the Catastrophe, Conservative Judaism, Summer 1964–The Face of God after Auschwitz, Sermons and essays, 1965–After Auschwitz 1966, Morality and Eros 1970–Jewish Faith and the Holocaust, 1969, the People Israel Live, The Christian Century 1970, Jewish Existence and the Living God, Commentary, August, 1969, and God's Presence in History, 1970.

[93] God in Search of Man, John Calder, London, 1956, p. 377.

[94] Seymour Cain, The Question and the Answers after Auschwitz, Judaism, Summer, 1971, pp. 263-278.

[95] Harper and Row, 1970.

which had agitated alert minds. When Nachman Krochmal's magnum opus, Guide of the Perplexed of our Time, was published in 1851 it gave contemporary Jews a better understanding of Jewish history as well as of religion, and it helped them to discern the future.

Jewish existence has undergone fundamental changes since 1933. First, there was terrible silence after 1945. Then the silence was broken. The Holocaust generated restlessness and interest. Young and old, believers and secularists, simple and educated people wanted to know the whole truth. Silence is no longer possible. It would spell blasphemy. For believing Israel, as well as for civilized humanity, the Holocaust is not just another mass murder. It can hardly be compared with any of the massacres in Jewish history for the last two thousand years.

The naturalist principle that man is the measure of all things has been shattered by the experience in our own age. Modern man is more profoundly perplexed about the nature of man than his ancestors were. It is therefore natural that he should turn to the question, "What is the measure of man?" Nazi ideology and German genocide of European Jewry must be judged not only by what it accomplished, but also by what it did not succeed in doing. It seems that it requires time to develop a religio-theological philosophy of the Holocaust. Our age is crying out for a new Guide for the Perplexed, and we hope that it will come sooner rather than later.

The American rabbinate, by and large, felt the need to study and interpret the Holocaust. Attempts were made, from time to time, to meet the growing awareness of the six years of horror, which culminated in the annihilation of Six Million Jews.

For instance, on April 9, 1964 a Conference was held in Memory of the Six Million, at Park Avenue Synagogue, New York, under the chairmanship of Jacob Agus. Excellent papers were presented by Seymour Siegel, Max Gruenwald, Jacob Agus, Isaac Toubin and David Silverman.[96] J. Agus, A.J. Karp, A. Ungar, A. Hammer, and most eloquently, R. Gordis, followed up the Conference by writing about and interpreting the experience of the Holocaust. I am deeply indebted to Gordis for his interest in questions which I have frequently raised.

[96] Conservative Judaism, Summer, 1964, Vol. XVIII, No. 4.

Eugene B. Borowitz notes in "Hope Jewish and Hope Secular," "that the Holocaust caused no mass desertion from Judaism but, on the contrary, resulted in deliberate commitment to Jewish values and to the survival of the Jewish people. This goes to prove that outrage at the Holocaust stems from a profound and indigenous moral sense."[97]

Imaginative Literature (Poetry and Prose)

Artists, poets and novelists, next to historians, political scientists and religious philosophers have long ago recognized that the comprehension of the chimneys of Auschwitz contains a key to understanding our century and our place in history. Poets and novelists have the unusual privilege of "licentia poetica." People are often fascinated by a poet or novelist. They will read poetry and novels, and accept fictitious scenes uncritically, as well as rhetorical questions as facts. Particularly, documentary novels are very popular nowadays. This makes the fourth aspect of the Holocaust literature the most difficult part to evaluate.

Whenever the poet and novelist describe scenes of annihilation, they should remain within the confines of historicity and authenticity. No matter how beautiful their language and how impressive their style might be, they too, must be guided by the general principles of historiography. This does not mean to imply that their poetical or novelistic imagination should be in any way curtailed. However, misleading statements in a novel are undesirable because the reader accepts them at their face value. They might lead to oversimplifications and misunderstanding. The poets and novelists, too, must remember that they are walking on holy ground.

Space limitations do not permit one to cite more than a few examples. Elie Wiesel, Michael Elkins, Yehiel De Nur are very popular and their novels permit us to illustrate the point.

Over the last decade Elie Wiesel has established himself as one of the most prominent Jewish novelists of our generation. His fiery style and piercing analysis of "man's inhumanity to man" give his books a special meaning. Wiesel's novel, "One Generation

[97] Jewish Spectator, September, 1972, p. 21.

After," is no exception.[98]   Novelist Wiesel personifies the Holocaust in a unique way. His uniqueness embraces rare qualities of a
talented writer, the gift of a penetrating observer and the pathos
of an ethicist, all at the same time. He is in a way the Jeremaiah
and Yehuda Halevi of our generation. While Wiesel's prose is
poetry, his philosophical observations are full of mysticism. He
speaks with the voice of a haunted saint, with the passion of an
abandoned prophet. All these qualities of the author make his
works classics of Holocaust literature, but they don't justify
statements which are based on oversimplifications or lack of
knowledge of European and German political and social history.

Like many haunted greats before him, Wiesel constantly returns
to the central theme. He writes in his novel: "We shall never
understand how Auschwitz was possible."[99] In a lecture delivered
in Los Angeles in May, 1968, "The Fiery Shadow—Jewish
Existence out of the Holocaust," Wiesel phrased it differently:
"We still don't know why and how a people, a whole people,
turned overnight into murderers and all accomplices to murder,
while another people, almost a whole people, almost overnight,
became the victims."[100]

The "Why" and "How" are recorded in German history and the
"Overnight" is an oversimplification. Hitlerism, the policy of
extermination against the Jews, the Slavs and others has its
intellectual forerunners in Paul de Lagarde and Houston Stewart
Chamberlain. The former described in "Deutche Schriften," the
plan and the steps which would lead to the elimination of Jews.
The Slavs would have to make space for the Germans by retreating
to Central Asia. Alfred Rosenberg, chief Nazi ideologist, praised
"the nobility of Lagarde," comparing him to Frederic the Great
and Bismarck. Heinrich von Treitschke introduced the super-race
theory academically.[101]

---

[98] Random House, New York, 1970.

[99] p. 128.

[100] Anderson, Ritchie and Simon, Los Angeles, 1970, p. 41.

[101] His influence on German mentality was baneful. So was his anti-semitism. He
predicted the enslavement of the Slavs by the Teutons. "The Teuton, a born conqueror,
takes his property where he finds it." Peter Viereck, Metapolitics, The Roots of the Nazi
Mind, Capricorn Books, New York, 1961, p. 204.

Race superiority, the harvest of hate, and the hunger for
domination, methodically prepared in the 19th century, ideologically cultivated by the Nazis, was only partly surprising. Hitler's
aims were threefold: integration of all Germans, world domination
and extermination of the Jews. He encountered no real opposition. The collaboration of the German people and Volksdeutche
everywhere, and the connivance of the Wehrmacht; the benevolent
passivity of Western Europe in the 1930s, the reaction of the
Soviet Union to Munich, causing suspicion, all these led to World
War II. The S.S. troopers marched singing: "Today Germany
belongs to us, tomorrow the whole world." Streicher addressed
the party congress in Nuremberg, September 1936, proclaiming:
"It is wrong to believe that the Jewish question can be settled
without bloodshed; the only possible solution is a bloody one."
Hitler predicted the annihilation of the Jewish race in Europe in
the Reichstag, on January 30, 1939: "Today I want to be a
prophet again." The result of another World War will be "the
annihilation of the Jewish race in Europe!"

Wiesel repeats observations and reiterates statements which he
has made in previous books and essays. An observation encountered in his previous writings is the comparison of Auschwitz
and Jerusalem. The author writes:

"Israel, an answer to the holocaust? It is too convenient, too
scandalous a solution. To pretend that without Auschwitz there
would be no Israel is to endow the latter with a share of
responsibility for the former."

Wiesel defends in his books—as well as in the Los Angeles
lecture mentioned before—the thesis that "nothing would be a
greater blasphemy than to say that Israel is the answer to
Auschwitz. What was undone in Europe, has not been returned
and reunited in Jerusalem. These are two separate mysteries. These
are two distinct events. To impose a logical sequence on
Auschwitz and Jerusalem, or a design other than dialectical, would
be to diminish both."[102]

Michael Elkins is a journalist by profession. He is stationed is
Israel, works for BBC and writes for Newsweek. However he wrote
"Forged in Fury"[103] over a period of eight years, because of his

[102]One Generation After, p. 128.
[103]Ballantine Books, Inc., New York, 1971.

personal involvement in an idea and commitment to a cause. The survivors of the Holocaust whom the author met in Israel, convinced him that strong men will resist evil under all circumstances and seek afterwards to punish the evildoers. The writer has a powerful pen which he uses frankly and unconventionally.

"Forged in Fury" is a powerful account of Jewish resistance during World War II, and the hunting and prosecuting of War criminals in the post-War period. The historian will read Elkins' book with reservations, as a mixture of history and fiction, until the two are separated.

The author writes in the Foreword: "I have changed some names, some dates and places; I have invented some details. I have done this to protect the people involved and enable their work, of which I approve, to continue." Elkins' fiery book quotes data, figures and facts based mostly on official reports of the Allies as well as on memoirs and works published in the last two decades by Americans, Israelis and Europeans.

The third phase of Elkins' interesting book deals with the post-War period. A group of soul-burned survivors formed a group of avengers, called DIN, meaning judgment. DIN is an acronym. Elkins writes, "There is a Hebrew phrase, a fighting slogan going back to biblical times: Dahm Y'Israel Nokeam—The blood of Israel will take venegeance."[104] I am assuming that "Nokeam" is a printing error and it should read "Nokeym." The author has created the impression that this "Hebrew phrase" is either a quotation from the Hebrew Bible or some other source going back to "Biblical times." It must be stated that this is not the case!

However, it is regretable that Elkins did not research the episode about an alleged meeting between Malachi Wald and Chaim Weizmann at Rehovot more thoroughly. He writes: "There is no record of their meeting, only what Wald remembers. It must have been a curious one ..." Wald visited Palestine seeking approval of a fantastic plot to poison the water supply of an entire German city. He sought the help and endorsement of the Hagganah. The plot ended with Wald's arrest by the British as a result of "betrayal," presumably by the Hagganah. The Hagganah disapproved of the plan.

[104] Ibidem, p. 193.

Yehiel De Nur is today an Israeli. Bert Meyers is an American. A. Anatoli (Kuznetsov) is a Russian-Ukrainian. Meyers' poems, "The Dark Birds,"[105] Kuznetsov's "Babi Yar"[106] are classics. Kuznetsov's "Babi Yar" is beautiful and authentic. Meyers is a Californian, self-educated, an authentic Jew, and gives evidence of unusual talent. Their novels and poetry are both inspiring and helpful in understanding suffering as related to the Holocaust disaster. So is Yehiel De Nur's Star Eternal, Katzetnik 135633.[107]

The Nazis invented and developed—among other things—the idea of the concentration camp. However they called it "Konzen-tration Zenter," literally: concentration center. An inmate of a Konzentration Zenter, initials K.Z. was known as Ka-tzetnik. Each Ka-tzetnik had a number, branded into the flesh of his left arm. The blue number became a symbol that one was permitted to enter the camp invented by the super race. The author of Star Eternal is Ka-tzetnik 135633. He is also the author of a remarkable best seller, House of Dolls, which is a Holocaust classic and was translated into twenty-two languages. It is quite under-standable that a writer describing his experience at Auschwitz should use a number as his pseudonym. At the concentration camp he had no name. It was left at home on Park Street, in a metropolis, somewhere in Poland. He was only a number at Auschwitz.

The last few pages of the booklet are entitled: Wiedergut-machung. One of the characteristics of the German language is the ability to coin long words. It takes three words in English to translate: "Wieder-gut-machung," literally: "Making-good-again." The author writes: "Mother, now they want to give me money to make up for you. I still can't figure out how many German marks a burnt mother comes to." "Of all mothers in the world, mine was the most beautiful. On her way to the crematorium my mother saw my face. I know it. Because I, too, on my way to the crematorium, saw my mother's face."

Ka-tzetnik 135633 indicates that he wants no part of the "Wiedergutmachung." Many survivors accepted restitution. Others refused to be bribed. Frankfurter Rundschau, February 24, 1953,

---

[105] Doubleday & Co., New York, 1969.

[106] Farrar, Straus and Giroux, New York, 1970.

[107] Translated by Nina De Nur, Arbor House Publishing Co., Inc.

described the restitution as a profitable deal, and Dr. Thomas
Dehler, Minister of Justice of the Bonn Republic, said: "The
settlement with Israel is a business for which the Americans will
compensate us handsomely." And they did.

The poetry related to the Holocaust is multilingual. It expresses
various moods; softness and bitterness, tenderness and determination, history and fate, the timely and timeless. Above all, it
demands answers to unanswerable questions. The poets described
sorrow. They eulogized, lamented, protested against God and man;
rebelled against society, and asked questions. They wrote in
Hebrew, Yiddish, German, Czech, Polish and many other languages. Among the poets were non-Jews as well. A special sense of
mission unites them all; mainly the desire that the tragedy should
not be forgotten. Future generations will have to read these poems
because history cannot afford amnesia. The purpose of dealing
with poetry and mentioning the names of a few poets should call
our attention to a simple fact: that they deserve a prominent place
in the Holocaust Literature. The Jewish poet reacted emotionally,
regardless of whether he wrote his poems in Jerusalem, Stockholm, New York, Warsaw or Terezin. Some of the poems were
written by children. They too wanted to know why God was
hiding His face and what happened to man.

Yitzhak Katznelson cried out in a poem, "I dreamed a dream,"
written on August 24, 1943. The poet had a nightmare:

        I dreamed a dream
        A very frightening;
        My people is not,
        My people is not anymore.

This poem sets the tone and describes a dreadful reality. David
Shimoni, Jacob Fichman and many others joined him. However
they were fortunate because they lived in Palestine. Katznelson
was sent to Auschwitz from a concentration camp in France,
where he perished.

The Nobel Prize winner, Nelly Sachs, is a great poet of the
Holocaust. She had been awarded the Droste-Hulshoff poetry
prize in 1960 and the Peace Prize of the German Book Trade in
Frankfurt, 1965. The Frankfurt Peace Prize is awarded for
"encouragement for the conception of peace, and understanding
among peoples." Nelly Sachs was fortunate to flee to Stockholm
with her mother in 1940. The Swedish novelist, Selma Lagerloef,
made their escape possible. The rest of their family perished in
Germany.

In a poem addressed to survivors Nelly Sachs wrote:

> We, the rescued,
> Beg of you:
> Show us our sun slowly.
> Let us step by step from star to star.
> Let us live again.[108]

Jacob Glatstein symbolically described the poetry of the Holocaust as "Memorial Poems" ("Gedenkenlider"). When we speak of Holocaust literature we usually refer to books which were written in prose. The poets within it are generally ignored or given only a second place, if at all. Of two recent studies, The Anthology of Holocaust Literature published in 1969, has very little to say about the poetry related to the tragedy, although the same Jacob Glatstein was one of the editors of the anthology. Irving Halperin's Messengers from the Dead, Literature of the Holocaust, published in 1970[109] has almost nothing to say about the poets of the Holocaust, while the author has given a great deal of attention to Victor E. Frankl's experience and thinking in concentration camps.

Halperin dismissed the Holocaust poetry when he wrote: [110] "They are, of course, some important Holocaust poems and plays such as the poems of Nelly Sachs, Jacob Glatstein, Yitzhak Katznelson, and the plays 'The Deputy,' 'The Investigation,' 'The Condemned of Altona.' But a few stars do not a constellation make . . ." Even if it were true that the poems can not stand alongside such classics created by Elie Wiesel, Emmanuel Ringelblum, André Schwarz-Bart, Chaim Kaplan, Rolf Hochhut, and Victor E. Frankl, they are nevertheless unmistakably filled with a deep sense of mission and deserve to be recognized as such. Of course Frankl's contribution to the understanding of the tragic life in the extermination camps is very valuable, but within the psycho-philosophical realm of the discussion.

Mordecai Gebirtig saw his town in flames. Gebirtig wrote:

> Our town is burning, brothers burning.
> Any moment the fire may

---

[108] Midstream, March, 1967, p. 18.

[109] The Westminster Press, Philadelphia.

[110] Ibidem, p. 20.

Sweep the whole of our town away;
And leave only ashes black and grey.[111]

Children, among them Pavel Friedmann wrote at Terezin an unforgettable poem, "The Butterfly." He was eleven years old. Eva Picková was twelve years old when she wrote the poem "Fear."

My heart still beats inside my breast
While friends depart for other worlds
Perhaps its better—who can say?
Than watching this, to die today? [112]

Wadyslaw Broniewski, a non-Jew, eulogized his compatriots in a poem: To the Polish Jews:

No cry of despair rose from Polish cities and towns.
The defenders of Warsaw's Ghetto fell like a gallant
    battalion.
A wandering Polish poet, I steep my words in blood
And my heart in a deep sea of tears
To write of you, oh, Polish Jews.[113]

Hava Rosenfarb summed up the despair of Holocaust poets, of many lands and tongues, when she wrote:

So I wait for Him—
Blind and lame
Deaf and dumb
In my windswept tent.
That He should lead me to a prayer
Somewhere in a corner of a town
Or in the middle of a field,
Or on a mountain top—
Waiting, I shiver in the cold . . .[114]

As time goes on some of the poets and novelists will find their rightful place in our liturgy and prayerbooks. If we remember the most gruesome tragedy of our history and its victims at the Synagogue on solemn occasions, we bear witness to the truth of Judaism and the greatness of mankind.

[111] Anthology of Holocaust Literature, Jewish Publication Society, 1969, pp. 38-9.

[112] I never saw another butterfly, McGraw-Hill Book Co., New York-Toronto-London, p. 45.

[113] Anthology, Ibidem, p. 373.

[114] Conservative Judaism, Summer, 1966, p. 25.

2

God and

the Holocaust*

The inquiry into the Holocaust and God's silent role in it originated in Palestine immediately after 1945. Long before Elie Wiesel's passionate Din-Torah with God and his piercing accusation of the entire world,[115] the radical theology of Richard L. Rubenstein, and his psychoanalytical interpretation of God in Auschwitz. It began before the soothing theodicy of Emil L. Fackenheim and the learned explanations of Samuel E. Karff about the Aggadah and the problem of evil and suffering. Theologians, writers from all walks of life, Rabbis representing all branches of Judaism, addressed themselves to the greatest of all evils. Among others Jacob B. Agus and Seymour Siegel presented papers on the theological and philosophical aspects of the Shoah. The challenge and the perplexity of the catastrophe was discussed at a special conference. Lately Robert Gordis elaborated on the

*Reprint from Judaism, V. 20, No. 3, Summer 1971.

[115] Elie Wiesel, The Legends of Our Time, Holt, Rinehart and Winston, 1968.

subject in a lecture in Los Angeles at a Convocation which dealt with the meaning of Jewish Existence.[116]

These writers are trying to come to grips with the imminent meaning and far-reaching religious implications of our recent tragedy. When World War II ended and the results of Cannibalism became known, historians and theologians began to interpret its meaning, and this process of grappling with the catastrophe still continues. It is fair to summarize the Holocaust theology as having alarmed our dormant conscience and having raised pertinent questions without bringing us closer to an acceptable answer. Victor E. Frankl quotes Lessing who once said: "There are things which must cause you to lose your reason or you have none to lose."[117]

Why then are we, Jews, trying to reason, analyse, rationalize something as ugly, pervert and evil as the Holocaust? We must continue with it for two reasons: Firstly, a Jewish people and a Judaism which survived at the price of ignoring Auschwitz would not deserve to survive.[118] Secondly, because if we Jews don't keep on reminding the world of the atrocities, humankind will soon forget it completely and deny that it ever happened. We are duty bound to search relentlessly and painstakingly. It is an encouraging sign that mankind has not forgotten. Neither Jews nor Christians can afford to ignore Auschwitz. Civilized people must grapple with the problem continuously and meticulously. The human impulse in mankind is the hunger for the impossible, the unattainable, the inconceivable. Anything which is less than this is not worthy of the name, glory and existence of the human race.

---

[116] Richard L. Rubenstein, After Auschwitz, Bobbs-Merrill, Indianapolis, 1966.

Emil L. Fackenheim, Jewish Faith and the Holocaust, a fragment, reprinted by Atid, New York, from a Commentary article, 1969, and The People of Israel Lives, a reprint by the American Jewish Committee, New York, from the Christian Century Article, May 6, 1970.

Samuel E. Karff, Aggadah—The Language of Jewish 'God-Talk,' Judaism, Spring, 1970, pp. 158-173.

Jacob B. Agus, Seymour Siegel and Others, Conservative Judaism, Summer, 1964, pp. 2-50.

Robert Gordis, Jewish Existence in an Open Society, Anderson Ritchie and Simon, Los Angeles, 1970, pp. 5-17.

[117] Man's Search for Meaning, Beacon Press, Boston, 1963, p. 18.

[118] E.L. Fackenheim, Jewish Faith, p. 2.

Theodicies
Thesis—Antithesis—Synthesis

If we are to continue with theodicy as a religious philosophy of traditional monotheism, then the following three alternatives are open to us. The first is Fundamentalism, whose exponents believe that man cannot always grasp the mysteries surrounding him. In this respect there is no disagreement among traditionalists of all faiths. In the past Jewish theologians wrote poetical and philosophical theodicies to explain and justify the ways of God to man.

If Godhood means both omnipotence and omniscience, then why does He permit evil to exist, whether caused by man or nature? Why did He permit the most atrocious crimes to be planned and executed by the Germans while civilized people worshiped in Churches, mosques and synagogues? Our forefathers, too, were perplexed as they realized and observed the existence of evil. Jeremiah's (ch. 12, 1) outcry was heard in the Land: "Why is the way of the wicked prosperous?" The question echoed and re-echoed in the ears of the faithful. "The righteous suffering and the wicked prospering?" was recognized as the problem of the day.

Today it is fashionable to discuss how meaningless is the fundamentalist point of view. It is, indeed, unacceptable to the "educated and mature" mind, but, the fact remains that some well educated, mature and pious men still adhere to it. Their piety and faith are stronger than reasoning. The traditionalist simply declares that God's ways are inscrutable and there is no point in trying to find the reasons behind them. Though His ways may appear unjust to our faulty perception, they are not really so. The fundamentalists claim that man is good, but suffers from an insufficiency of both knowledge of what God expects of him and of genuine reverence and "fear of the Lord." Elie Wiesel quotes a Hassidic saint, who said: "For the faithful there are no questions for the non-believer there are no answers."[119] Does this mean that the "sophisticated" believer, who believes and questions, has no place in the congregation of the faithful?

[119] Jewish Existence in an Open Society, ibidem, p. 41.

Philo, following Plato, identified God with goodness and absolved Him of evil. The process of creation, according to him, means the revelation of God's goodness and bringing order out of chaos. The world is the scene of an endless struggle against evil, but without it the creative process would cease. Man has body and spirit and combines both evil and good. Philo omits the fact that man commits evil not only with his body, but also with his mind. Whether the analysis of evil, its origin and operation, is helpful in facing it is a moot question, and will be determined by the personal temperament, background and orientation of the individual.

Educated, and religiously committed, Jews will derive comfort from Judaism. It recognizes our world as still in the making, and our moral obligation, unique opportunity, to participate in its betterment. Despite all difficulties which we encounter today, even the critic has to admit that the world responds—partly—to our effort and thought. There can be no nobler mission in life than to join those who make such an effort.

Mordecai M. Kaplan writes: "Not a single one of the numerous theodicies, or attempts of thinkers to reconcile the goodness of God with the existence of evil, has ever proved convincing."[120] The modern, educated mind will not accept the Holocaust as the result of our sins, or of an unexplainable mystery. Kaplan notes that it is not surprising that none of the great minds from Samson Raphael Hirsch to Leo Baeck and Martin Buber came up with a satisfactory solution of the problem of evil.[121] Neither can an adult mind accept Herman Cohen's explanation that "misery and pain are needed in order to awaken the conscience of men and thereby to advance the cause of ethical progress." "Evil is the necessary background of good; it is the chair for the good," and "evil appears evil to our limited understanding." Cohen also has the answer as to why the poor suffer. "The suffering of the poor is a kind of sacrifice for the sins of all mankind . . . as the price of progress. It is the saints that suffer. God loves the miserable." [122]

[120] Judaism as a Civilization, Reconstruction Press, New York, 1957, pp. 115, 329, and Questions Jews Ask, Reconstructionist Press, New York, 1956, p. 116.

[121] Questions Jews Ask, Reconstruction Press, New York, p. 118.

[122] Jacob B. Agus, Modern Philosophies of Judaism, Behrman's Jewish Book House, New York, 1941, pp. 108-111. Compare W.T. Stace, Time and Eternity, An Essay in the Philosophy of Religion, Princeton University Press, New Jersey, 1952, pp. 56-60.

In other words: the nicest children of God are to pay the price for all of us.

We are introduced to the second alternative by Richard L. Rubenstein and his radical theology. Contemporary Judaism and the American Jewish Community have been exposed for the last decade to theological radicalism. Rubenstein is a disciple of Mordecai M. Kaplan whose religious philosophy (naturalism) influenced his thinking. However, he has drifted away in the last decade from the founder of Reconstructionism and become closely identified with Thomas Altizer. Paul Tillich praises the German philosopher Nietzsche, who proclaimed that God is dead.[123] Rubenstein claims that in face of the German [124] atrocities, only two answers are possible in regard to the Holocaust. Either we accept the "traditional answer" that Hitler was used as an instrument of bringing divine visitation upon the Jewish people—or we must assume that "God is dead." His pessimism concerning our civilization is based on psychology and the inability of man to discipline himself. Freud's pessimistic predicament about human potentialities[125] dominates Rubenstein's philosophy when he writes: "The fantasy of a world without restraints, the world in which God is dead, can be imagined at many levels."[126] He uses the "Auschwitz rhetoric" rather eloquently.[127]

I confess my regret that a promising, almost brilliant, mind has not found a different language to convey his message. I might eventually understand that Rubenstein by joining the ranks of contemporary Protestant radical theologians has sentenced God to die,[128] but I cannot understand why he continues to disturb Him? To describe "God after-the-death-of-God" as "Holy Nothingness" or the "omnipotent Nothingness is Lord of creation," tells the reader nothing at all, certainly about Nothingness.[129]

---

[123] Richard L. Rubenstein, After Auschwitz, p. 87.

[124] I prefer to use "Germans" instead of "Nazis" and my preference is based on L. Poliakov's statement mentioned in this essay.

[125] After Auschwitz, p. 89.

[126] Ibidem, p. 36.

[127] A phrase used by Jacob Neusner, Midstream, October, 1970, p. 72.

[128] After Auschwitz, p. 243.

[129] Review of his book: Morality and Eros, in Midstream, October, 1970, p. 73.

As we study the books of Jewish theologians of previous generations dealing with the eternal quest, men who were critics, dissenters and innovators from Maimonides to Kaplan, we hear soft and God-inspired voices: Divrey Elohim Hayim, Words of a Living God. Except for the Karaites, who were involved in theological as well as personal polemics with the Rabbanites, Jewish theologians always were soft spoken whenever they disagreed with their predecessors or contemporaries. Whether Harvey Cox is right that "the rise of urban civilization and the collapse of traditional religion are the main hallmarks of our time" remains to be seen. Only the future will tell to what extent any contemporary theologian or thinker was right or wrong. One thing is sure, that Rubenstein the theologian, radical, original and often brilliant, has decided to travel the road to a "very private subjectivity." He has made some friends and gained some followers, but he has also galvanized the great majority of American Rabbis to a condemnation of his Auschwitz and Post-Auschwitz rhetoric. Surely, there must be better ways in which a Rabbi can express his dissent from his own teachers as well as from those of the past.

The third alternative in pursuing the idea of resolving the dilemma of evil and suffering generally, and the Holocaust particularly, is Rationalism. Robert Gordis in his early writings introduced the Biblical concept of theodicy with special emphasis on Job and Deutoro-Isaiah.[130] He reiterates and expands this idea in The Book of God and Man—A Study of Job and in the new edition of A Faith for Moderns. The Justification of God in a world of undeserved suffering is based on a socio-theological analysis of the Biblical text, and Gordis introduces into his theodicy two doctrines which, when combined, represent a "realistic and more compassionate" answer.

The first, often expressed in the Holy Scriptures, is the idea of the mutual, moral interdependence of man. Men are organically related to one another. Therefore, when some men sin, other men suffer. Mankind is like the human organism. Each individual organ, can and will, influence the well being or the aching of the whole

---

[130] Judaism for the Modern Age, Farrar, Straus and Cudahy, N.Y., 1955, pp. 228-36, and particularly the essay on the Book of Job in Great Moral Dilemmas, Harper and Brothers, 1956, pp. 155-178. A Faith for Moderns, Bloch Publishing Co., New York, 1970.

body. The Germans[131] committed monstrous crimes and the Jews became the victims. Not God, but the Germans brought suffering and inflicted it upon Jews and others.

The second doctrine of "vicarious suffering" is found in the writings of the Prophets, particularly in Deutoro-Isaiah. "When one loves another human being, one is bound to suffer with and for the loved one."[132] Humankind is likened to a family, and a crime committed by one of the members will cause anguish and pain to all other members no matter how innocent they are.

Let us assume that we follow Gordis approvingly to this point and accept his rationale. Our difficulty remains how to explain it to the educated but Jewishly uncommitted Jew. Why were we Jews chosen to suffer for Europeans, most of whom had failed to stand up and to be counted. The annihilation of one and one half million innocent Jewish children can hardly be explained by vicarious suffering alone and will not satisfy the critic; neither will it help to explain why innocent Biafran children had to die because Africans failed to act rationally. Although we perpetuate tradition, we must realize that we are not living in an age of the Prophets who spoke to their generation in a Prophetic language but were nonetheless often discouraged, for their contemporaries simply did not understand them. Only if we find our own semantics and the ability to speak of, and about, the Holocaust in our own language will we find some satisfaction and, eventually, an answer to this very agonizing question.

Irrelevance of Theodicy

The problem of theodicy is as old as Judaism itself, or as Religion, for that matter. Joseph Klausmer defined the theodicy of the Holocaust as the "question of all questions" and Klausner admitted that Jewish thinkers of all ages found answers but not "the answer" to the question of why the righteous suffer and evil exists.[133]

---

[131] León Poliakov in Harvest of Hate, Syracuse University Press, Syracuse, N.Y., 1954, p. 8 and p. 156, writes: "... genocide, because it affects the deepest levels of man's spirit, cannot be carried out without the concurrence of all the people."

[132] Robert Gordis, Jewish Existence in an Open Society, p. 14.

[133] The Question of all Questions and Answers, in Mibayit, Agudat Hasofrim Haivrim B'eretz, Yisrael, Tel Aviv, 1946, pp. 7-30.

As we enter the second quarter of a century of research—theological, philosophical and historical—into the problems of the Holocaust, the question is being raised whether our tragedy should be considered as a theological or a socio-political problem.[134]   It would be quite reasonable to expect that man today should behave differently from his less educated and less sophisticated ancestors of thousands or even of hundreds of years ago. But reality tells us that man only sometimes behaves better than did his forefathers, and often does not. Man has failed to make of man a better human being. It looks as if God left this educational opportunity to humans, and they have failed to take advantage of the opportunities which are theirs. In the words of Erich Fromm, "Man's life is determined by the inescapable alternative between regression and progression, between return to animal existence and arrival of human existence. Any attempt to return is painful, it inevitably leads to suffering."[135]

Louis M. Shifier, a gentile who was an inmate of a concentration camp, wrote in the Israeli Davar, in 1961 "that one can write about War, even if one has not participated in it, but it is impossible to write about concentration camps unless one has lived in one."[136]

Two men survived in concentration camps: one, Elie Wiesel, speaks of "a mystical dimension" when he writes, "We still do not know what took place there, let alone why certain events took place there the way they did."[137]   The other, Victor Frankl, being a psychoanalyst, uses the "existential dimension" in discussing the psychology of the Concentration Camp. He writes, "While the outsider was too far removed from the strange world of the concentration camp and could scarcely empathize, the person who was in the midst of it had grown hardened to its laws and had no distance. It can therefore be said that we have no adequate description of just what took place since we have to allow for a considerable degree of distortion in the mentality of the

[134] Trude Weiss-Rosmarin, The Jewish Spectator, October, 1970, p. 31.

[135] The Sane Society, Fawcet Public, Inc., Greenwich, Conn., 1965, pp. 31-3.

[136] K. Shabbetai, As Sheep to the Slaughter, World Association of the Bergen-Belsen Survivors Association, New York, Tel Aviv, 1963, p. 46.

[137] Elie Wiesel, Jewish Existence in an Open Society, p. 41.

viewer."[138]   In a letter addressed to Robert Gordis after his
lecture given in Los Angeles in May, 1968, I wrote in part:

> The purpose of my letter is two fold. Firstly, permit
> me to call your attention to the fact that the question
> of "God is dead" was raised by American rabbis and not
> by survivors of the Holocaust. It is, therefore, mislead-
> ing when you state that "one can not only understand
> but empathize with those who, having gone through the
> hell-fires of Nazism, continue to feel the iron of persecu-
> tion in their own being and are therefore unable to
> accept any rational approach to this darkest of all
> riddles." This sentence creates the impression that the
> "God is dead" theology came from the ranks of the
> survivors while, indeed, the rabbis who introduced it
> into American Judaism lived thousands of miles away
> from the scene of the crime. They, then, and not the
> survivors, are responsible for this discussion of theodicy
> in Judaism. This is a fact which ought to be stressed
> clearly.
>
> I lived in Budapest from February, 1942 until June,
> 1948, and spoke to a goodly number of Rabbis, (not
> only from Hungary, but from Central and Eastern
> Europe, as well), who had returned from concentration
> camps and I don't remember any of them making God
> responsible and declaring Him dead because of the
> inhumanity of the Germans and others.
>
> It is true that these survivors asked questions and
> revolted, too, but they rebelled against society, rather
> than against God. Their rebellion was against the socio-
> political system which tolerated "man's inhumanity to
> man." Some of them became leftists and preachers of a
> new socio-political order, but they did not challenge or
> deny the existence of God.

I confess that I find the following individuals, who survived the
Holocaust, to be more profound as spokesmen of Auschwitz than
are the writers of radical theology.

---

[138]The Doctor and the Soul, Bantam Books, New York, Toronto, London, 1969,
p. 75.

Rabbi Yekutiel Yehudah Halberstam of Klausenburg lost his wife and eleven children at Auschwitz. When asked whether he still believed that the Jews were the Chosen People he answered, "That precisely then, after all that had happened to him and the Jewish people, had he been confirmed in his belief in the choseness of his people, because it was not the Jews who had committed the acts of horror, but the gentiles . . . "[139] Victor E. Frankl, founder of the Third Viennese School of Psychotherapy, writes: "One cannot claim that these men (i.e. concentration campers) had undergone a regression; on the contrary they experienced a moral progression—moral, and religious. For there broke out in many a prisoner in confinement, and because of confinement, what I have designated as a subconscious or a repressed relationship to God. Let no one judge this religiosity disparagingly, or dispose of it as 'foxhole religion . . .' In any event, many prisoners came forth from prison with the feeling of having learned to fear nothing except God."[140]

It seems that our generation will be divided between those who experienced, through the Holocaust, the "hiding of God," and those, who feel that the "hidden God" was absent in Auschwitz and elsewhere, because He was dead. We might do well to be reminded of the parable of the Hassidic saint, Rabbi Baruch, who tried to explain the game to his grandson who was playing hide-and-seek with another boy. He hid himself and stayed in his hiding place for a long time assuming that his friend would look for him. Finally, he went out and saw that his friend was gone, apparently not having looked for him at all. Then he ran to his grandfather complaining about his friend. Hearing the story Rabbi Baruch broke into tears and said: "God, too, says: 'I hide, but there is no one to look for me.' "[141] Or to put it in other words, "The problem of religion is precisely the problem of one's supreme loyalty of devotion."[142]

[139] K. Shabbetai, ibidem, p. 36.

[140] Psychotherapy and Existentialism, Simon and Schuster, New York, 1968, pp. 99-100.

[141] Abraham J. Heschel, Man Is Not Alone, The Jewish Publication Society of America, 1951, p. 154.

[142] W. Herberg, Judaism and Modern Man, The MacMillan Company, New York, 1951, p. 371.

Eva Picková, a twelve year old girl, in the camp at Terezin, wrote a poem entitled, "Fear." The last stanza reads:

> "No, no, my God, we want to live,
> Not watch our numbers melt away.
> We want to have a better world,
> We want to work—we must not die."[143]

The inscription on the walls of a cellar in Cologne, Germany, where Jews were hiding from Nazis, touches the hearts of many, while contemporary radical Jewish theologians appeal only to a few. How inadequate is the statement and the comparison that "Judaism and Christianity are in the process of becoming neo-archaic, pagan religions in fact if not in name," as compared with the mentioned *inscription:* "I believe in the sun even when it is not shining. I believe in love even when feeling it not. I believe in God even when He is silent."[144]

Mordecai Bar-On, head of the education program of the Israeli Armed Forces once wrote, "I belong to the generation which was born without faith. When I read the literature about the Shoah my reaction is, 'I shall not die, but live.' I say to myself, what can I do in response to this horrible act? My answer is to strengthen my faith in, and my attachment to, Judaism."[145]

[143] The Artists of Terezin, by Gerald Green, Hawthorne Books, Inc., Publishers, New York, 1969, p. 172.

[144] Anthology of Holocaust Literature, The Jewish Publication Society of America, 1969, p. 340.

[145] Petahim, Elul, 5727.

3

Unanswered

Questions

A. Anatoli (Kuznetsov) wrote in Babi Yar, "If civilization is in danger today, if it is fated to decline and perish, it will do so with the enthusiastic assistance of credulous people. They seem to me more dangerous than the most brazen leaders, because everything is done with their co-operation. Meanwhile their numbers are becoming depressingly large . . . "[146] One of the severest critics of world Jewry is Elie Wiesel. Wiesel stated, both in public lectures and in articles, that world Jewry abandoned European Jewry. "Never before have so many Jews been abandoned by so many Jews." Then he continued: "When consulted by their governments whether to bring in refugees, some communal leaders had to answer, and their answer was less than enthusiastic."[147]

These statements are directed against the American Jewish Community as well as against Jews in the free countries of Europe.

[146] Farar, Straus and Giroux, New York, 1970, p. 392.
[147] Judaism, Summer, 1967, p. 282.

Elie Wiesel in a talk (Holocaust Memorial Day Observance, 1972) recently charged the American leadership with silence and failure. They failed to come to the aid of the Jews in Nazi concentration camps and forced ghettos. "They did nothing," he said. "Why didn't they go mad?" "How many marched on Washington?" "How many tore their clothes in mourning?" "How many weddings took place without music?" Then he continued: "Why did not the French march into the Rhineland in 1936?" Jewish Telegraphic Agency Executive Vice President, Jack Siegel, immediately wrote a meaningless apology, to discharge the burning soul of Elie Wiesel and to exempt the Jewish leaders from the guilt syndrome. The politics of rescue under the Roosevelt administration is a bleak chapter in American history. Jewish leadership cannot be exonerated from the indictment. The American archives have been opened and no apology, no matter how well written, can help us.

The Jewish Voice of Los Angeles printed a letter to the Editor, on June 16, 1972, which expressed the sentiments of survivors in a meaningful way. The criticism leveled at the Jewish Telegraphic Agency and Mr. Siegel is justified, to say the least.

"Editor:

I was burning with anger after having read Mr. Siegel's article. I am a holocaust survivor having outlived the death camps and the Warsaw Ghetto. I am the only survivor in my whole family and I was deeply disturbed by the attitude of this Jewish leader.

The past cannot be erased and a helpful lesson should be learned for the future.

It is now clear that Jewish as well as non-Jewish leaders had an idea about what was happening in the European ghettos. Unwillingly Jewish leadership along with world leadership silently conspired to the situation and did not bring across the message of the Jews' plight to the world community.

European Jewry thought they were being taken to work camps and hoped to outlive this hardship. They never knew until late 1943 of the real nature of the camps—death. While other imprisoned nationalities received moral support in the form of broadcasts and encouragement the Jewish leaders remained silent. The Jewish Telegraphic Agency was among the silent parties and therefore was called "The Silent Voice."

American Jewish sons and daughters who served in the army did so to defend their own country, their own skin; not to save the ashes of European Jewry.

If Jews had known that their lives were at stake they would have defended themselves just like they did when the camps' objectives became known in 1943. Millions could have been saved just by broadcasting available information.

Mr. Siegel either doesn't know the facts or purposely falsifies them. For example the gas chambers were purposely designed for Jews. No nation of the world lost 1/3 of its people. Most of the others lost their lives in a war where they at least had an opportunity to defend themselves—to kill or be killed. No nation of the world had 6,000,000 casualties who couldn't defend themselves. No other nation has so felt the impact of genocide. To put the war dead and the gas chamber deaths together means to falsify history and to present a distorted picture to the future generations.

Did Mr. Siegel know that any music in Auschwitz was an irony? All those designated for death were presented with a concert before death. When a group was "enjoying" a concert we knew that their time had come.

I do not believe that mourning and prayers could have saved European Jewry, nor did "Joint" packages ever reach the Jews. I unloaded these packages for the Germans. But on the other hand, demonstrations in Washington or at least some militant action or public broadcasting could have saved numerous lives.

I am happy to see enormous involvement by American Jews and World Jewry on behalf of Russian Jewry and Israel. An important lesson should be learned. Let's keep history correct no matter how much it hurts so our children and our children's children can learn a lesson from it. Yours, Max M. Kronen."

There are many unanswered questions. Some are related to man, others are theological in nature. Instead of answers to these agonizing questions we encounter apologies. These questions are related to the victims, their brothers and friends abroad, their close neighbors in the occupied territories and compatriots. It was customary in Talmudic times after an exhaustive discussion of a difficult problem, to which the Rabbis found no answer, to rest the case by stating: "In due time, when the Messianic age will usher in, the answer to the question will be forthcoming." These unanswered questions are:

How could all this happen in the enlightened twentieth century? How was it possible that Christian nations reverted to such savagery? Why did the Germans support Nazism after its leaders openly declared the extermination of the Jews? Why did the Balts, Rumanians, Hungarians, French, Greek, all Slavs, and even the Italians, collaborate with Hitler's hordes? Where were the powerful Churches, both the Roman Catholic and Protestant, and why did they fail to intervene?[148] Could the Jews abroad have done more than they really did? Could the governments-in-exile have exercised more pressure upon the Allies and their military leaders? Where were the Soviets and the partisans in the East? Where were Central and Western Europeans during the crucial years? Could they have done more in helping Jews and admitting them unconditionally into their ranks? Where were the Socialists and Communists among the Germans and Austrians? Could the Palestinian Jewry have played a more active role during the crucial years? And above all could the European Jews, in the occupied lands, have resisted? Could the Jewish leaders of Europe have forseen the catastrophe? Could they have prepared the Jewish masses to resist the Germans and their collaborators? Was the Jewish faith in God an obstacle and their belief in Man a deterrance in the struggle for Survival? And finally: Is it humanly possible to forget and to forgive the Germans? Did only the Nazis or did all other Germans also cooperate in the "Final Solution"? Where were the neutrals (Spain, Portugal, Sweden, Switzerland, Ireland) until 1944? Did the International Red Cross intervene wherever it could have done so? Why was civilized mankind silent? In the course of reading the judgment which found Eichmann guilty Chief Justice Landau also posed the following questions: "How could this happen in the light of day, and why was it just the German people from which this great evil sprang?" "Could the Nazis have carried out their evil designs without the help given them by other peoples in whose midst the Jews dwelt?" "Would it have been possible to avert the catastrophe, at least in part, if the Allies had displayed greater will to assist the persecuted Jews?" "Did the Jewish people in lands of

---

[148]The Greek Orthodox Church is an exception. In the first place Greek Orthodox Church leaders were often oppressed, too. Secondly they were by a long shot not as powerful and influential as the Vatican, or its contra part in Protestantism. Thirdly, they have established a much better record, at least in some of the pro-Axis countries, than did the two other branches of Christianity.

freedom do all in its power to rally to the rescue of its brethren and to sound the alarm for help?" "What are the psychological and social causes of the group hatred which is known as anti-Semitism? Can this ancient disease be cured, and by what means?" "What is the lesson which Jews and other nations must learn from all this in regard to every man's relationship to others?" This is by no means an exhaustive or complete list of all unanswerable questions. It is long enough to keep us occupied for some time to come if we are to answer them.

Has the second half of the twentieth century created an atmosphere more conducive to justice in the world? Do we experience a greater respect for the human personality? Is progress only an illusion? In the course of a dialogue about progress, Bernard Shaw's sphinx comments impassively that as long as it has been there, a matter of a few millenia, it hasn't noticed much progress.[149]

For the last three millenia at least Prophets, Sages and Saints dreamed that humanism will emerge. They believed that man can be transformed because he is not merely a zoological specie, but a unique creature. We have experienced in this century "history" which refutes all this. Buber quoted the young Scipio in a paraphrase: "Just as we take our horses back to the trainer at the end of a campaign, so after every political victory we should again submit to the discipline of the philosopher, lest we lose touch with humanitas." Konrad Burdach wrote in an essay, analyzed by Buber, that "the greatest desire Nature has implanted in every thing from its beginning is the desire to return to its origin." Furthermore the goal of humanism is "to return to the human origin, not by way of speculative thought, but by way of a concrete transformation of the whole of inner life."[150]

Is our age concerned with humanitas at all? It manifests itself, to be sure, in all corners of the world, even in places and at times where the belief that peoples as well as individuals could be transformed was not cultivated. The possibilities of educated men to believe in the future of mankind are actually limited. The rediscovery of freedom makes political philosophies, which limit our freedom physically or intellectually, unacceptable to man, who wants, above all, to be free. The personal price which

---

[149] A. Anatoli, Ibidem, p. 264.

[150] Israel and the World, Ibidem, p. 242 and p. 244.

totalitarianism imposes upon the individual is too high, and the uncertainty to what it might lead, too risky. Democracy has a long way to go to deliver the promises and to fulfill the hopes which the term entails. The crisis in Western societies, as well as in non-Western undergoing modernization, is in keeping pace with and becoming relevant to a longing for a genuine democratic way of life.

The confrontation between history and modernity has led to a radical situation, at least on the American stage. Thomas Altizer tells us with the solemnity of a confessional pronouncement that "we must realize that the death of God is an historical event, that God has died in our cosmos, in our history, in our Existenz." [151] Herman Kahn and Anthony Wiener predicted that the twentieth century cultures will continue to be increasingly "empirical, this-worldly, secular, humanistic, pragmatic, utilitarian, contractual, epicurean or hedonistic, and the like." [152]

Nobody has the power of prophecy, not even the radical theologians. But one thing we know to be sure, that humanism must at all events be humane and not consist of concentration camps and gallows. Until man has been transformed into humanitas "we must strive for nothing less than the concrete transformation of our life as a whole. The process of transforming our inner lives must be expressed in the transformation of our outer life, of the life of the individual as well as that of the community. And the effect must be reciprocal: the change in the external arrangement of our life must be reflected in and renew our inner life time and again."[153]

When this will be accomplished, then man will "not do unto his neighbor what is hateful unto him." Following the footsteps of the prophet Malachi (2, 10), who cried out, "Have we not all one father? Has not one God created us?" the Rabbis continued (Taanith, 18), and added, "Are we not brothers of one father and one mother? Why are we singled out for inhuman oppression?" The sublime admonition to mankind, regarding the Fatherhood of God and the brotherhood of man, is as relevant today as it was more than twenty-four centuries ago.

[151] Thomas J.J. Altizer and William Hamilton, Radical Theology and the Death of God, Bobbs-Merill, Indianapolis, 1966, p. 11.

[152] The Year 2000—A Framework for Speculation on the Next Thirty Three Years, MacMillan, New York, 1967, p. 7.

[153] Buber, Ibidem, p. 245.

4

Lesson for
Humanity

Wars create many problems yet solve very few. The most difficult and painful of all are: the disregard for human life and the lack of justice. Once life has returned to normal and man begins to think about good and evil, he is also absorbed in rebuilding cities, in removing the ashes and in eradicating ruins. He soon forgets the evil and the evildoers. Ethicists have said it for a long time, that sympathy is a human virtue. "Thus by means of the sympathy[154] aroused at the sight of social injustice, the religious man is enabled to perceive his fellow-man in every human being." Sympathy, "Mitleid," is the source of the feeling of human solidarity.[155] However, sympathy has its limitations. "Human sympathy . . . is forever limited in the world of existence

[154] In Greek: syn—together and pathos—suffering, feeling.

[155] Jacob B. Agus, Modern Philosophies of Judaism, Behrman's Jewish Book House, New York, 1941, p. 108.

because I can only know my neighbor's suffering through my imagination. I can never truly suffer with him as I ought, if I am to understand him."[156]

This could be one way of explaining why civilized humanity has paid relatively little attention to the suffering of the Jewish people during, and immediately after World War II. The Vietnamese, the Biafrans and the Bengalese went through an experience of suffering and received only our limited sympathy. They, too, must have felt a deep sense of disappointment in man's ability to sympathize with his fellow-man. Hermann Cohen wrote about "Mitleid" concerning the religious man. I hasten to add that a man need not be a practicing religionist to feel anguish and unhappiness when he encounters cruelty and suffering anywhere in the world. With the exception of certain rodents, no other vertebrate habitually destroys members of its own species. No other animal takes positive pleasure in the exercise of cruelty upon another of its own kind.

War is evil, an evil which results in destruction and ultimately in death. Our first impulse, as humans, is self-preservation. War leads to self-destruction. In the tragic competition and confusion of interests in which every race, continent, nation, ethnic group and social class is caught the distinction between right and wrong, between good and evil, even when clearly defined and easily visible, is not necessarily acceptable to the parties concerned. The commitment to lasting peace will eventually emerge as a result of human experience, knowledge and deep conviction that peace is "the categorical imperative" of the "holy dimension of all existence,"[157] and the only road to human survival. Once man reaches the moral stage and says, "I would rather excel in the knowledge of right than in the extension of might," then peace will be his, even without the presence of an arsenal of nuclear weapons. There is a sign of hope. Man is capable of discovering wisdom in disaster. It is a long, evolving process, which is both painful and full of zigzags.

[156]Jacob Kohn, The Moral Life of Man, Philosophical Library, New York, 1956, p. 51.

[157]Abraham J. Heschel, Man is not Alone, The Jewish Publication Society of America, 1951, p. 237.

For us today as well as for those of tomorrow the following story has relevance. Two philosophers were once discussing the history of mankind. Said the first philosopher, who was a pessimist, "All History of Mankind may be summarized in four words—Man's Inhumanity to Man." The second philosopher, who was an optimist, replied, "No, my friend. The four words that summarize the history of the human race are: 'From Suffering to Wisdom.'" Anyone who would have dared to predict, forty years ago, that a German Chancellor would advocate a peace treaty with Poland and the Soviet Union in 1972, although it meant giving up German territory, would have been called a madman.

The ancient Hebrews had a passion for justice. Their children, exiled from their homeland, suffered immensely because of Wars. Sociologists and historians claim that one hundred million Jews have lost their lives because of wars and persecution in the last nineteen hundred years. Man's natural happiness is love accompanied by justice and peace. Our future will be secure when we begin to do justly, to act mercifully and to walk peacefully. These are the well-springs of our life and should govern our existence.

Religion has taught for millenia, and science has proven it, that Justice means fairness among equals. Whether or not we admit it, we feel instinctively that all men are equal. Judaism and monotheistic religions stress Mutual Responsibility, Moral Interdependence and the Pursuit of Justice as the keynotes for human survival. The process of evolution instructs us in not only knowing how to live, but in knowing how to live together to build a better future. Man is gradually learning to understand not only the identical direction of all human aims but the natural goals of all human life. According to Jewish tradition, God has created but not completed the creation of the world. For the world is not yet finished. There is much important work to be done before it is complete. God is dependent upon us, the human beings, to be his faithful co-workers. To be co-workers with God means to eliminate the imperfections in the unfinished structure of the world. It means trying to make it a more secure and beautiful place in which to live. Among the Jewish sages of our time, Mordecai M. Kaplan [158] states that "if we cannot believe in the potentialities of human

[158]Questions Jews Ask, Reconstructionist Press, New York, 1956, pp. 124-5.

nature, we have nothing on which to base our faith in the goodness of God." But "progress is not automatic. Advances in one direction may be accompanied by decline in others." Kaplan speaks of God as "the Power that makes for righteousness and salvation." Kaplan writes: "The first person to have hit upon this idea and to have discovered that this idea was the distinctive contribution of Hebraism to world civilization, as distinct from Hellenism, was Matthew Arnold. He summarized that idea in the phrase 'God is the Power that makes for righteousness—not ourselves.' By 'not ourselves' he meant to say that righteousness was not a human convention but a law inherent in the very nature of reality."[159]

Other modern thinkers like Henry Nelson Wieman, for example, are inclined to identify God with the evolutionary process; insofar, at least, as this points in the direction of man's further humanization and self-fulfillment.[160] If one is reluctant to subscribe to such concepts of God as "Power" or "Process", then one ought not lose sight of the fact that the goal of life is not sudden perfection but the "ever-enduring process of continuing, enduring, refining," as John Dewey pointed out. Peace may not be around the corner because of many factors. The answer to man's deepest need is still far off. May God grant that we do indeed become the masters and not the slaves of man's accumulated wisdom and experience. It is now man's highest and most urgent obligation to educate himself to face life, opportunity and the future with the deepest sense of moral responsibility.

Leo Baeck wrote, in the essay entitled "God and Man in Judaism," that reverence toward man implies and underlines an aspect of the principle—"the conception of history and human responsibility for it. Man is in humanity and for it." Baeck elaborated the relationship between an individual people and humanity in a chapter entitled "The Encounter with God." "Any people cannot, may not, be without humanity or beyond humanity. God questions humanity through the people. Humanity lives only through these people, those that have come into being and those that are in the process of becoming. Every people is thus

[159] The Purpose and Meaning of Jewish Existence, The Jewish Publication Society, Philadelphia, 1964, p. 324.

[160] Jacob Kohn, Evolution as Revelation, Philosophical Library, 1963, Foreword.

responsible for the fact that humanity exists . . . A people exists, just as the individual exists, when he is conscious of responsibility and finds his life in it."[161]

S.S. Cohon summarizes the teachings of Judaism and the modern view of evil when he writes "perfection, both personal and social, is not something ready for us to be found, but something to be attained and acquired. Man is a portion of the unfolding world. Its ends are partly realized through his cooperation . . . What invests man's moral, spiritual and intellectual striving with true significance is the solidarity of the human race. Closely related to one another, the acts, achievements and failures of one individual affect all the rest. If we benefit from the labors of our forebears and contemporaries, we are also compelled to expiate their misdeeds as well as our own . . . We bear the burdens of wars, though we individually have no responsibility for their occurrence . . . It follows, as Royce pointed out, 'that in our moral world, the righteous can suffer without individually deserving their suffering, just because their lives have no independent Being, but are linked with all life.' "

All humans are laborers in the garden of life where hardship and dangers go hand in hand. Ethical and social refinement make us more sensitive to and aware of pain, misery, injustice and selfishness. Endless changes have taken place in the realms of politics, science and technology. Our world is not only changing, but also growing more complex. Life threatens to become too strenuous, too manifold, too involved. There is growing evidence that progress in industry and technology, in science and politics alone cannot insure the welfare of the individual and of society. The growth of ethical and social values is needed, but is missing badly. Such dimension would help humanity to rise above defeat and to establish the laws of righteousness, goodness and truth. By virtue of our mental endowment, mankind plays an active role in the world drama. We suffer more than the animals because we feel more keenly than they do. We see more around us and often ahead of us, than the animals, because we think, analyze and understand. "To be on the side of the forces that make for an increase of good over evil, of justice over wrong, and of brotherhood over strife is

[161]This People Israel, Ibidem, p. 395.

its own reward. Despite all obstacles, life may flower forth into ethical and spiritual perfection."[162]

Peace is the vision of something which stands beyond, behind and within the passing of every generation. It is an idea which is real, and yet waiting to be realized. It is something which is a remote possibility, and yet within our reach; something which is the ultimate ideal, and the hopeful quest. Although peace has eluded us, it remains the hope which gives meaning to all that passes, to our existence today and our plans of tomorrow. It is a prophetic dream of a world governed by a moral order.

[162] Judaism A Way of Life, Schocken Books, New York, 1962, pp. 64-7.